Chrysalis Reader

ORIGINAL ESSAYS, POETRY, AND SHORT STORIES
ILLUMINATING THE WORLD OF SPIRIT

VOLUME 10

DEBORAH FORMAN
PUBLISHER

CAROL S. LAWSON & ROBERT F. LAWSON
SERIES EDITORS

ALICE B. SKINNER
ART EDITOR

SUSANNA VAN RENSSELAER
ASSOCIATE EDITOR/LAYOUT DESIGN

ROBERT TUCKER
FICTION EDITOR

ROBERT F. LAWSON
POETRY EDITOR

MARY LOU BERTUCCI/PATTE LEVAN/PERRY MARTIN
CONTRIBUTING EDITORS

RICHARD BUTTERWORTH
EDITORIAL ASSISTANT

KAREN CONNOR
COVER DESIGN

FOTO SEARCH
COVER ILLUSTRATION

PART PAGES ART
MARGOT TORREY

New England artist MARGOT TORREY creates woodcuts using pine planks cut to length for a small print destined for a calendar or a long board carved and printed on cloth for a banner. Torrey says, "I like the tactile quality of the art and the energy transmitted from the heart and hand, through gouges and knives to wood, and then with ink to paper."

PUBLISHER'S STATEMENT
The Chrysalis Reader is a journal of spiritual discovery published in honor of Emanuel Swedenborg. Eighteenth-century scientist, civil engineer, and mystic, Swedenborg used his scientific orientation to explore the world of spirit. Respectful of all lives lived according to faith in the divine, Swedenborg described the ever-present reality of the spiritual world.

Eternal Wellness

THE IMPORTANCE OF HEALING, CONNECTING,
COMMUNITY, AND THE INNER JOURNEY

Eternal Wellness

THE IMPORTANCE OF HEALING, CONNECTING,
COMMUNITY, AND THE INNER JOURNEY

Edited by Carol S. Lawson & Robert F. Lawson

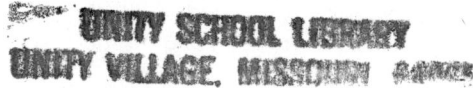 CHRYSALIS BOOKS / *Swedenborg Foundation Publishers*

THE CHRYSALIS READER is a book series that examines themes related to the universal quest for wisdom. Inspired by the writings of Emanuel Swedenborg, each volume presents original short stories, essays, poetry, and art exploring the spiritual dimensions of a chosen theme. Works are selected by the series editors. For information on future themes or submission of original writings, contact Carol S. Lawson, Route 1, Box 4510, Dillwyn, Virginia 23936.

©2003 by the Swedenborg Foundation

All rights reserved.

No part of this book may be reproduced or transmitted in any form or by any means, electronic or mechanical, including photocopying, recording, or any information storage or retrieval system, without prior permission from the publisher, except in the case of brief quotations embodied in critical articles and reviews.

Printed on recycled paper and bound in the United States of America.

LIBRARY OF CONGRESS CATALOGING-IN-PUBLICATION DATA
Eternal wellness: the importance of healing, connecting, community, and the inner journey / edited by Carol S. Lawson & Robert F. Lawson.
p. cm. — (Chrysalis reader; no. 10)
ISBN 0-87785-234-0
1. Spiritual life. I. Lawson, Carol S. II. Lawson, Robert F., 1948– III. Title IV. Series: Chrysalis reader; v. 10.
BL624.E88 2003
810.8'0382—dc21
                                                                                   2003011794

CHRYSALIS BOOKS
Swedenborg Foundation Publishers
320 North Church Street
West Chester, Pennsylvania 19380

Contents

EDITOR'S NOTE
Spiritual Compass: Aligning Body—Mind—Spirit ix
  Robert F. Lawson

PREFACE
Parable of the Well xii
  Paul J. Ruschmann

PART I: INNER JOURNEY
Single Kayak, Open Sound (poem) 5
  Steven Lautermilch
Values in Tension 7
  John L. Hitchcock
Tree Wisdom 13
  Sarah Quigley
Poem without a Category (poem) 18
  Suzanne Freeman
The Old Priest 21
  Paul Gordon
Housecalls: A Doctor's Spiritual Journey 27
  Richard Moskowitz
Expanding the Core 37
  Marilyn Kreyer
Pondside (poem) 40
  Wesley McNair
The Awakening 41
  Barbi Schulick
Reinventing Your Life's Mythology 47
  Dorothea Harvey
In Idleness (poem) 52
  Linda Lancione Moyer

PART II: HEALING
The Laughter of Wood (poem) 55
  Cal Kinnear
Good Body, Happy Man: The Uses of Life's Difficulties 57
  Wilson Van Dusen
Thoughts on Growing Younger 61
  Catherine Lazers Bauer
Silent Retreat 64
  Steven J. Moss
Go Ahead and Take Your Medicine 67
  Donald L. Rose and Michael Taylor

Culinary (poem) 72
   Wyn Cooper
Cooking as Meditation 73
   Jean Arnold
I arise like a doe in springtime (poem) 77
   Asher Pucciarello
Healing with the Breath of Life 79
   Andrew Caponigro
R'uach Ha R'uach (poem) 87
   Philip Lisagor
Landfalls 89
   W.E. Reinka
Love, Laughter, and the Nature of Life 91
   Bernie Siegel

PART III: RECONNECTNG

We Cannot Extinguish the Night (poem) 97
   Margaret Szumowski
The Manifold Manifestations 98
   Penny Susan Rose
William My Friend (poem) 109
   Vincent DeCarolis
The Decision 110
   Barbara Walker
Reunion (poem) 115
   Blayney Colmore
Druid Arch 117
   Lani Wright
Coyote Fool Moon 120
   Wendy L. Brown
Shakuhachi and the Alhambra (poem) 127
   Carol Lem

PART IV: COMMUNITY

Oranges (poem) 131
   Art Stein
Quiet Ponds 132
   M. Garrett Bauman
Bread (poem) 138
   Nina Romano
In the Blink of an Eye 139
   Richard Weinkauf
The Exit Tamer (poem) 148
   Tim Kahl
The Holy Virgin of Chernobyl 151
   David Zane
Quaker Peace Vigil 157
   Gary Sandman
Trust (poem) 161
   Thomas R. Smith

EDITOR'S NOTE: ROBERT F. LAWSON

Spiritual Compass

Aligning Mind—Body—Spirit

IN A THREE-DIMENSIONAL WORLD, one can move in six prescribed ways—forward, back, side to side, up or down. But when working in the spiritual realm, one must accommodate a seventh direction—going within. *Eternal Wellness: The Importance of Healing, Connecting, Community, and the Inner Journey* searches for the source of spiritual well-being following interior passageways that may at times defy logic, a map that includes heart and feeling.

Through essays, stories, poetry, and art, *Eternal Wellness* explores a variety of approaches to being spiritually centered, in alignment with the universe at large, in harmony with life, and in touch with our understanding of the spirit or life-force that flows through it all. Examine with one author the value of humor in healing. Follow another author's journey in which her spiritual practices "step over the line" and become part of a cult. Watch a retired professor reconstruct her personal mythology in order to adjust to a new self-awareness. For another, experience spiritual activism as part of a community of seekers holding a peace vigil. Discover how one woman's weekend vision quest enables her to attain a sounder mind, body, and soul.

In this issue we learn that for one person being spiritually grounded may mean to be seated beside a pond in predawn light, allowing troubling thoughts to settle. For another, it may mean stand-

> *Bodily peace is, of course, the health of the body... but besides health, there is also a delicious and perceptible peace of the whole body... an actual and perceptible operation of spirits into the inner organs of the body, in harmony with the original shaping of the internal organs.*
>
> —EMANUEL SWEDENBORG
>   1747, the 20th day of December
>   *Spiritual Experiences*

ing in line at the bank, meditating on the "breath behind the breath," tuning oneself to the heartbeat of the universe. Yet for someone else, it may mean moving mindfully alone among the massive sandstone outcrops of the Canyonlands.

A myriad of practices point to spiritual well-being and enlightenment, but which practices are for us, which ones to trust? Is it possible that one size fits all? *Eternal Wellness* examines the dynamic of spiritual balance, asking what constitutes a healthy diet of spiritual nourishment. Can one overdose on too much of a good thing? If there are teachable moments, how do we make the most of these moments? In one author's account, we travel with an older priest as he rides in an ambulance to Ground Zero. Trying to maintain his connectedness—integrating love, self-doubt, and duty in his work with firemen and paramedics struggling around him—he questions, *When you feel ill in spirit, how do you seek healing? Who serves as your spiritual doctor?*

For those who persevere, *Eternal Wellness* suggests that the answer will come from inside. In my case, as I have been dealing with bladder cancer while working on this issue, guidance has come in dreams. During my first hospitalization, I dreamed that I dove from the prow of a hospital ship. As I swam in the ocean, a school of dolphins overwhelmed me. I was frightened, seeing their open mouths and teeth. They simply engulfed me, and the king of the dolphins said that he had adopted me, that I was the prince of dolphins. Together we pressed on, inhaling, churning the ocean white, attacking the cancer, expelling the toxins.

In the end, perhaps there is no right path, no prescribed route through pleasant valleys and pristine mountains. Instead, one might just as likely find devastated fields and rugged chasms—with no guardrails. We must discover for ourselves which spiritual practices, which guideposts, speak to us and, with heightened senses on alert, knowing there are tantalizing possibilities waiting for us within, follow with courage and trust in our heart.

Opposite:
David Wynne.
Girl with Dolphin.
Bronze, 1974.
Pepsico
World Headquarters,
Purchase, New York.

PREFACE: PAUL J. RUSCHMANN

The Parable of the Well

FAR OUT IN THE DESERT, beyond the last oasis, there was a little well. Dry and in a deplorable state of disrepair, it looked as forlorn as the dunes in the moonlight. One day a solitary traveler, a pilgrim carrying only a small bundle and a walking staff, stopped at the little well to rest.

"The pilgrim must be lost," thought the well, "for no one ever comes out here anymore. Soon this one will leave, for only a fool would stay, knowing my well is dry."

But the pilgrim stayed.

The little well had been nearly swallowed by the desert after many years of neglect. The pilgrim unpacked the small bundle and started to clean the sand and dust from around the base of the well. Smoothing the ground with bare hands, the pilgrim removed so many pebbles and stones from around the well that a low wall was built, protecting the little well from the sudden siroccos and keeping the constantly shifting desert sands at bay. The pilgrim then replaced the frayed rope, patched the holes in the leaky bucket, and oiled and polished the rusty crank. Though the pilgrim's supplies were meager, there was nothing that was spared in bringing the little well back to life. Taking some seeds from the bundle, the pilgrim planted them around the well in what remained of the sandy, sun-bleached grass.

In no time—though it could have been days or weeks—the once-abandoned oasis sparkled and shone in the sun. A flag fashioned from the pilgrim's colorful scarf flapped proudly in the breeze. Anyone who came to the farthest oasis now and saw the little well glinting in the sun and its colorful flag flapping in the breeze would think that it was one of the most beautiful in the entire desert.

Opposite:
Camille Pissarro.
Peasant Digging.
Crayon on paper,
44.3×29.4 cm., 1890.
Art Gallery of Ontario,
Toronto. Gift of Sam
and Ayala Zacks, 1970.

Paul J. Ruschmann

But still, the well was dry.

"All this work was for nothing," thought the little well. And then, so moved by all that the patient pilgrim had done for it and saddened by the thought that the pilgrim would soon leave, the well began to cry.

The tears that had been held back for so long began as a trickle, and then a fountain, bubbling deep within the dark depths of the well. For what seemed like forever—though it could have been only minutes or hours—the little well cried. A puddle became a stream, and the stream became a spring as the tears of thankfulness and sadness poured out of the little well. Soon, there was the sound of gurgling and the splashing of water from deep within the well.

The pilgrim, who had been tending the dying plants with the last drops of water from a nearly empty water pouch, ran anxiously to the edge of the well and listened. A smile split the pilgrim's dusty, sunburned face. The bucket was lowered into the well, and time and time again, it came back drippingly full of sparkling, pure water. The pilgrim drank and drank of the cool, clear water and then, breaking into song, danced around and around the little well, watering the thirsty plants.

In no time at all—although it could have been months or years—the last oasis turned green and lush with the trees and flowers planted by the pilgrim. From these came a bountiful harvest of fruits and vegetables, of plums, figs, dates, olives, coconuts, and pomegranates.

From that time forward—every minute of every hour of every day of every year—there was so much happiness at the farthest oasis that the little well stopped crying tears of sadness and cried forever tears of joy.

PAUL J. RUSCHMANN, from Grand Rapids, Michigan, and a graduate of Aquinas College, has been published in the *Catholic Digest, Liquorian,* and *Public Libraries,* as well as in numerous local publications. "Writing is a passion. I agree with William Stafford, who once said that writing was something that he 'could not NOT do.' Photography and drawing as well as walking (for fresh air, exercise, and the companionship of one red dog named Ruby) take up some of my spare time. I follow the wisdom of Emerson and have made the public library my university."

Eternal Wellness

THE IMPORTANCE OF HEALING, CONNECTING,
COMMUNITY, AND THE INNER JOURNEY

PART I

Inner Journey

*At every step of our journey,
divine providence focuses on our eternal state.
It cannot center on anything else
because divinity, being infinite and eternal,
is not in time
and sees the whole future as present.
Thus, due to the nature of the divine,
it follows that something eternal
is in everything it does,
overall and in detail.*
—EMANUEL SWEDENBORG
   Divine Providence (paragraph 59)

STEVEN LAUTERMILCH

Single Kayak, Open Sound

Marsh of stars.
Each stroke of the blades, pulling down moonlight.
Horned owl, calling on shore.

Under the polestar, a lopsided diamond, a chubby dolphin
    of leaping stars.
Job's Coffin.
A kite on its side, a shell of light, a tail star in its wake.

Earth no longer made of land, buoys no longer in hearing
or sight. Only water now, ripple and wave
the breaking of night.

Poet and photographer STEVE LAUTERMILCH lives on the Outer Banks of North Carolina where he offers workshops in dream study, meditation, and writing. He is the author of eight chapbooks of poems, three of which have won national competitions. His artist's book, *Spirit Writer,* appeared last year, a sequence of poems and photographs centering on ancient Native American rock art. Selected photographs from the work have been displayed at the University of Nevada, Reno, the Duke University Clinic in Durham, and the Glenn Eure Gallery in Nags Head, North Carolina. Poems from the book have received the Luna Poetry Prize from CETOS and a Pablo Neruda Prize in Poetry in the Hardman Awards at the University of Tulsa.

JOHN L. HITCHCOCK

Values in Tension

I like to see it lap the Miles—
And lick the Valleys up—
And stop to feed itself at Tanks—
And then—prodigious step

Around a Pile of Mountains—
And supercilious peer—
In Shanties—by the sides of Roads—
And then a Quarry pare

To fit its sides
And crawl between
Complaining all the while
In horrid—hooting stanza—
Then chase itself down Hill—

And neigh like Boanerges—
Then—prompter than as a Star
Stop—docile and omnipotent
At its own stable door—

—EMILY DICKINSON
 The Poems of Emily Dickinson
 edited by R.W. Franklin
 Poem no. 383

Opposite:
N.C. Wyeth.
Winter "Death."
Oil on canvas, 1909.
Collection of Andrew
and Betsy Wyeth.
Photography courtesy
of Brandywine River
Museum. Chadds Ford,
Pennsylvania.

DICKINSON, ONE OF THE TOUGHEST PHILOSOPHERS OF THEM ALL, has done a magnificent job of describing values in tension. The train in Dickinson's verse was the great symbol of technological progress in her time. She catches our fascination with the image. At first we are caught up in childlike enthusiasm for trains or with the image of the journey evoked, and we don't notice such words as "supercilious," "complaining," or "horrid—hooting stanza." Dickinson's modern editor, Thomas Johnson, calls this poem a "biting satire on progress."

The poem leaves us with the tensions of "docile and omnipotent." Is the train (or the computer or nuclear power) godlike in its power yet docile to our commands? Is Dickinson referring to man, machine, or God?

Some people tend to identify technology as the source of a number of our civilization's problems while simultaneously enjoying and even demanding its benefits. Is the overemphasis on technology today leading to an unawareness of our spiritual selves? We have a dependency, not chemical, but a technological dependency. Every time we look at a watch and derive comfort from knowing the time, we get a technological fix. And there's the car, the TV, the CD and DVD, the computer and internet. With digital music and videos, we have added the symbol of digitization to our cultural enjoyments, our numerical fix with statistics and surveys. The world has become a clockwork mechanism.

But this only presents one side of technology. The compact disc can bring music into our lives with the power of a divine majesty. The CD can serve the spirit and thus serve meaning. The key to the effect or outcome of technology in our lives is not in the technology as such, but in our ability to choose how to use that technology and how we deal with its opposing consequences.

I believe that our principal means of psychological and spiritual growth lies in struggling with the tension of values. Such tension is an essential ingredient for finding spiritual well-being. If we are to grow and evolve as a species capable of caring for the planet entrusted to us, then we must recognize these opposing values and choose to respond with our own solutions, made visible in how we live. As we find the balance between what is practical and what is spiritual, we can center ourselves for choosing what action to undertake.

Daily life is full of paradoxes. We try to detoxify the environment, yet we fail to recognize our internal poisons. We identify with the highest human ideals and aspirations, forgetting that we humans are also egocentric and brutal. Without potentials for both good and evil, we would be moral automata, and our claim to be carriers or actuators of values of any sort would be meaningless. But we are not automata. There certainly is a higher power which helps us to desire and act for good and for love.

Once we accept the deep need for values in tension as a means of moving forward in the evolutionary process, it is then necessary to discover how to handle that tension nonexplosively, even in a very literal sense. We need to look newly toward the wholeness of reality; wholeness is precisely the holding or honoring of both values that come to tension in any given situation: individual versus social, self versus the other, masculine versus feminine, global versus local, etc.

THE NATURE OF OUR PHYSICAL AND SPIRITUAL REALITY is that all opposites are tied together, including moral light and darkness. Perfection, usually identified as separating out and cutting off all darkness from the remaining light, is therefore impossible.

We are generally unaware of our own inner darkness. We like to think of ourselves as relatively harmless. Although we often feel that others are unaware of their shortcomings, we fail to apply this logic as insight into our own blindness about ourselves. Psychologically, the process of seeing one's own faults as some other person's faults is called "projection." We project onto others not only our faults, but also our own potentials for greatness. This positive potential is also part of our shadow, a part of ourselves that we fear to face.

Thus, the shadow contains both our darkest and brightest sides. We get emotionally involved with figures of darkness in relation to world events, from Hitler to Osama bin Laden to Saddam Hussein, and want to rid the world of them. But each of us also has a desire to varying degrees to control others or a devotion to a rigid and narrow spiritual outlook. This is a centrally important principle with which to examine our lives. Ask yourself what are your strongest fascinations, both as attractions and as repulsions. What stirs your emotions? Whom do you envy? Whom would you like to remove from the face of the earth? If you make a list of such images, you can gain insight into your own character.

We also avoid facing our possibilities for greatness, which are often alarming to us. If we have plenty of money or a good job with security, it won't matter as much if we've not lived our potential. We know this is true, for we are attracted to reports on the rich and famous, quite apart from their moral characteristics.

Without darkness, freedom and self-awareness are impossible. We repress the consciousness of our inner darkness simply because we fear to face that part of ourselves. Sometimes it is a toss-up as to whether we fear more our "sinfulness" or our potential greatness. Either fear will keep us from awareness of inner moral conflicts or values in tension. But avoidance of the dark is also avoidance of the light, truth, wisdom, and the conscious relationship to inner powers that can help us. How often have we known people who have fallen into their inner darkness, "hit bottom," and who have been creatively transformed? Calamity can lead to deeper wisdom.

Cultural history has aided our self-deception. By teaching the "split," the "sheep-and-goats," or "wheat-and-chaff" view of humans. We have also perpetuated our self-deception by devising a system of punishments or of scapegoating (letting or forcing someone else to be the "dark being"). The tension contained in our darkness also can be relieved with scheduled release, as with Mardi Gras. We eagerly anticipate such times, knowing the feeling of really being alive that comes with them. If we really knew our dark sides, we might feel alive much more of the time.

We have been taught to strive for perfection by getting rid of our dark impulses. The Greek word *teleios,* which is used when Jesus is reported to have said, "Be therefore perfect, as your heavenly Father is perfect," is much better translated, "Be therefore complete, or whole," i.e., having no parts missing or including everything in your life which enters it. Indeed, this passage amplifies the point, as it says, "for [God] makes his sun to rise on the evil and the good, and sends his rain on the just and on the unjust." This great image of agricultural beneficence, which Jesus encourages us to emulate, should inspire us to find some way to be inclusive of our own darkness for the benefit in consciousness that it affords us.

Under any current ethic, we are all flawed in our living, causing feelings of guilt. Psychologists know that many children suffer from feeling that they "deserve" punishment that has yet to be visited upon them. Tendencies to undervalue ourselves are likely rooted in what we feel as unpunished guilt, carried from childhood into adulthood. Our "guilt" remains unreleased.

We continually attempt to revitalize the ancient Hebrew rite of scapegoating, prescribed as a ritual in Leviticus 16:20–21. In this ritual, the priest formally heaped the sins of the congregation upon the selected goat, which was then driven into the wilderness. For this ritual to work, people had to believe that the heaping of their sins was accomplished, requiring a naiveté that a modern education makes difficult if not impossible. Even in recent times, the punishment of criminals has enabled many people outside prisons to feel clean by projecting their own darkness onto those in prison. But it is our darkness that distorts our perception of our inner moral state.

Technology has also been a scapegoat, but the heaping of blame upon technology or upon political or economic systems hasn't worked, because it simply isn't true. We not only get what we deserve in the outer world—we get what we want. What will enable us to see and to admit this fact? If technology seems to us to engender a dis-relational world, the fault is ours in failing to bring relation along. We believe we want relationship with others and the world, but fear of the shadow prevents us from treading the necessary path.

Einstein is reported to have said: "We shall require a substantially new manner of thinking if mankind is to survive." I believe that this is to be found in "polar-inclusive" thinking (including polar opposites as equally valid in thinking about an issue). This thinking is based on "complementarity" as the great contribution of the new physics. As in the preceding example, darkness and light are both essential components of aliveness.

In physics, complementarity has survived rigorous scrutiny to become established as the new way of apprehending physical reality in its deepest manifestations. The idea of is that there are fundamental situations in which it is absolutely necessary to use contradictory concepts to achieve a complete or whole description of entities or phenomena. In these situations, the opposites cannot be separated because they apply to the same thing. This indicates that the opposites in general are subject to a higher unity; our own light and dark moral aspects are ultimately inseparable.

Although the shadow holds our inner darkness and collects our faults, it also contains our new life. Fear of our own shadow that has led us, individually and collectively, to the rigidities of our current psychic structure with its emotional defenses. This psychic energy builds to a bursting point because conflicting facts accumulate concerning our ideals that contrast with our actual behavior.

By recognizing our own darkness and withholding the projection of darkness onto others, we will automatically reduce conflict. In Neumann's terms, we become "non-infectious."* The benefit to ourselves is that we achieve a greater wholeness.

We cannot deal with our inner darkness purely intellectually. Emotions are involved, and thus we are on dangerous ground. We have a barrier layer of feeling, which prevents clear sight of facts until sufficient experience has been acquired or until we have run out of facile answers. If we are called to this kind of introspective work, sooner or later our inner contradictions make themselves known. To permit the inner tension that accompanies self-awareness is to become open to the very forces that drive our creativity.

I have tried to say as clearly as I could what changes we need to attempt in order to face our fears and guilt and thus have some real chance of hearing the creative Voice within. There is a wonderful bib-

---

*Psychologist Erich Neumann's *Depth Psychology and a New Ethic* deals with the application of C.G. Jung's concept of the "shadow" to ethics in daily living. When we recognize and take responsibility for our own dark side, we cease to infect others.

lical image (1Kings 19:9–13) in which the prophet Elijah experiences God in this way.

> And there he came to a cave, and lodged there; and behold, the word of the LORD came to him, and he said to him, "What are you doing here, Elijah?" He said, "I have been very jealous for the Lord, the God of hosts; for the people of Israel have forsaken your covenant, thrown down your altars, and slain your prophets with the sword; and I, even I only, am left and they seek my life to take it away." And he said, "Go forth, and stand upon the mount.". . . And behold, the Lord passed by, and a great and strong wind rent the mountains, and broke in pieces the rocks . . . but the Lord was not in the wind; and after the wind an earthquake, but the Lord was not in the earthquake; and after the earthquake a fire, but the Lord was not in the fire; and after the fire a still small voice. And when Elijah heard it, he wrapped his face in his mantle.

If such aloneness and divine charge were upon that prophet, why not upon any of us as well? After that powerful experience, God just sent him back to carry on his work. Before us passes a scene such as we can resonate with: it is as if our very life is sought by the powers of disintegration, and there is the tremendous clamor of winds breaking rocks, of earthquake and fire; all those tumultuous happenings, which may seem to us as divine judgments, even upon ourselves. But if we recognize and look beyond the fears that are symbolized in all the apparent upheaval, we may become quiet and hear a new inner voice. And what that voice will convey to us is the strength to endure and to work with values in tension.

JOHN L. HITCHCOCK holds graduate degrees in clinical mental-health counseling, phenomenology of science and religion, and astronomy. He has taught mythology and astronomy at San Francisco State University and physics at the University of Wisconsin at La Crosse. Since 1968 he has led seminars with the Guild for Psychological Studies of San Francisco, specializing in mythology and in science as a source of numinous symbols for personal growth and daily living. He is the author of *Atoms, Snowflakes and God: The Convergence of Science and Religion* (Quest Books, 1986), *The Web of the Universe: Jung, the New Physics, and Human Spirituality* (Paulist Press, 1991), *Healing Our Worldview: The Unity of Science and Religion* (Chrysalis Books, 1999), and *At Home in the Universe: Re-envisioning the Cosmos with the Heart* (Chrysalis Books, 2001). John is a clinical mental-health counselor. He and his wife Carrie are enjoying their new home in Topsham, Maine.

SARAH QUIGLEY

Tree Wisdom

IN MY EARLY THIRTIES, I decided to try my hand at freelance writing. Thirty-some-odd years later with five nonfiction books and over two-hundred articles, essays, and poems published, I survey my modest contributions with satisfaction. Currently, a skeleton of a novel hangs in my mind, with two chapters fleshed out, and there's at least one more nonfiction book that's beginning to take shape.

At the same time I was testing the freelance waters, my athletic mate began to coax me outdoors. I learned to ski, then took up jogging. It was fun shushing down a steep slope with my husband, who insisted he did not find me uncoordinated at all, even though initially it took me days to learn to board a chairlift. During warmer weather, I found it exhilarating to enter 10K races, knowing each entrant was struggling with his or her own challenges and not at all interested in critiquing my style of running or lack thereof. But deep inside, I remained an awkward little girl.

My main criterion for feeling safe in this world revolved around remaining invisible. When a staid friend admitted she fantasized about being a stripper, I stood with my mouth agape. I could never, ever, I thought, be comfortable in any kind of spotlight. Signing books at a bookstore was different. My work, much more than I, was on display. Although something I wrote might be criticized, I could almost certainly avoid being clumsy on paper.

In 1990, a set of puzzling physical symptoms appeared that frightened me, not just because they might be early symptoms of some grave disease, but because they were impossible to hide. While taking a long walk one day, I noticed my left arm hung limply, refusing to swing along with the right one. As I approached my front door, I felt my left foot dragging. Gradually other glitches appeared, and after consultations with two neurologists, I was diagnosed as having suffered a series of small strokes. It was only after symptoms began spreading to my right side that a correct diagnosis of Parkinson's disease was made in 1997.

Before I'd had a chance to tell her about my condition, my editor at Conari Press approached me to write a book about facing fear. I had no idea why this editor thought I could tackle this particular topic. But with a psychologist and friend, I began work interviewing people, conducting research, and drawing on my own experiences as I faced fears I could never have imagined confronting. The *Little Book of Courage* is comprised of two-page meditative essays. In the process of writing about how we all can face and feel our fears, then either transcend or transform them, I finally dared look at what had become a phobic fear about remaining invisible.

Although Parkinson's assorted symptoms vary with each individual, over a period of years, the illness becomes "noticeable." Before my diagnosis and a subsequent regimen of drugs that began to alleviate symptoms greatly, I was barely able to sign a check. My writing had become so small and shaky that I could no longer handwrite a letter or pen notes during a lecture. At the supermarket, or any place I planned to make a purchase, I made sure I had enough cash and always put the bills in the top of my purse, so I could grasp them without difficulty. If I got change back, I dumped it into my purse, so as not to attract attention to my fumbling fingers. If I needed a new pair of shoes, I shopped at the time of day when I was least fatigued—I didn't want a clerk clucking sympathetically as I struggled with the simple act of pushing my left foot into a shoe.

Once, in the mid-nineties, when I took an emergency flight to Atlanta to see my sick mother, I bristled when a well-meaning ticket agent asked if I might like to ride down the concourse in a wheelchair. I mumbled something about having gotten this far all by myself and turned away quickly to hide tears of embarrassment and frustration.

Almost two years ago, my medications, though still effective enough to keep me moving and functioning, began to cause dyskinesia—random involuntary jerky movements. So, while medications may continue to alleviate Parkinson's symptoms, they often begin to unleash their own St. Vitus dance. Mixed in with this hyperactivity, there often are "off" times when the medication has worn off and movement is laborious or impossible.

Human beings appear to be the most accomplished of the species when it comes to worrying about "how we appear." Since the onset of Parkinson's, I've spent lots of energy trying to concoct ways to keep looking good and not be deemed "ill" or "awkward." But how could I keep this swirling, tyrannical fear from shattering tranquility and stirring anxiety?

Opposite:
Alex Colville.
Elm Tree at Horton Landing.
Oil on masonite,
121.6×91.1 cm., 1956.
Art Gallery of Ontario, Toronto. Gift from the McLean Foundation, 1958.

Interestingly, at the same time that I have been dealing with my physical impairments, I've been increasingly drawn to nature for strength and for a different outlook. After glimpsing a terribly scarred tree, missing a huge limb, I wrote a poem as an emotional response to the experience. Here's the last stanza:

> I touched the textured hollow,
> thinking how trees go on offering,
> what they have, "as is," while we
> disguise flaws, camouflage signs
> of illness and decline, long to
> be as we were . . . but why?
> Must we go on caring how others see us,
> and, forever keep measuring,
> what was with what is now?
> In honor of tree wisdom, right there,
> I struck a yoga pose,
> teetering on one leg, tentatively
> raising the other to my thigh—
> my shaky imitation of a tree
> looked ridiculous—
> for the first time,
> my awkwardness
> was of no consequence.

Several years ago, I recalled a life-defining incident—a backyard scene with my father. One afternoon, tagging along after him—I must have been four—I got tangled up in my own two feet and crashed to the ground. I imagine I expected to be scooped up and comforted, but any such hope vanished when he mumbled, "You're the big-footedest little girl I've ever seen." His words stung more than my skinned knees. I remembered wiping blood off my knees, trying to restore my aplomb, as tears began streaking my dirty cheeks. But this time, I felt something entirely different from embarrassment. There was a flash of anger. *Why, Father, couldn't you focus on me for just a moment—talk to me, hug me, acknowledge me?* And then, remembering his thin, lined face, I felt a flood of compassion, feeling almost as if I stood in his shoes. How many of us get so beaten by circumstance and entrenched in habitual patterns that we develop a blind spot, ignoring one of our sacred duties? I know I have.

Since reconsidering that distant episode, I no longer feel hellbent on remaining unnoticed. When the day came to deliver a dear friend's eulogy, I wasted no time wondering who would notice or not notice my illness. This was, after all, about him, not me. And this past

September, I was able to respond to an invitation to travel to Vermont to read a series of my poems at the tenth anniversary celebration of the ToDo Institute, an educational retreat devoted to teaching several Japanese spiritual and psychological traditions that promote responsible actions, gratitude, and mindfulness. The dyskinesias were really bad that day, but I stood at the podium, reading words I hoped might inspire a few who had come.

My spiritual well-being hinges not on becoming free of Parkinson's symptoms or free from the dyskinesia but on not setting myself apart or staying behind closed doors because of embarrassment and self-consciousness. A time may come when this disease will actually curtail my comings and goings. Meanwhile, there is no need to either predict or impose restrictions prematurely.

Recently, while walking along the seawall on Galveston Island, my medication rather abruptly stopped acting, and I could feel the sinking sensation one who has Parkinson's can get when not enough dopamine is firing its signals to the part of the brain that commands our movements. I felt like a windup toy that was rapidly unwinding.

Carefully, I crossed the wide boulevard, walked into a MacDonald's, and ordered a "senior" coffee, ice water, and an egg MacMuffin. By the time I dragged myself to a booth, I felt a million years old. With effort, I pulled my medication dispenser from my jean's pocket, popped a little compartment open, and swallowed two pills. Then I sat waiting for their effects. Every so often a dose fails to work. I sat in the booth a full twenty minutes, hoping I could walk the mile back to our condominium. My contingency plans were to call a cab. I had enough cash in my pocket.

I won't lie. This incident scared me. But this time the fear led to practical solutions—I had only to figure out what to do and not become sidetracked, wondering what anybody else might be thinking about a rather stone-like figure of a woman sitting in a booth, letting her food get cold. The medicine kicked in. I wolfed down my breakfast and not only walked back, but also stopped in Wal-Mart to pick up a few groceries. I was within a block of my condominium when a stiff headwind came up along with a light rain. A passing motorist, a woman, shouted, "Want a ride?" I told her I was almost home.

And I was.

SARAH QUIGLEY is daily endeavoring to cultivate her own courage and is working on a new book about that topic. A collection of her poems and her husband Jack's black-and-white photographs, entitled *Nature's Healing Presence,* are periodically on display in a gallery on the Strand in historic downtown Galveston, Texas. Sarah and Jack divide their time between Galveston and Gainesville, Georgia.

SUZANNE FREEMAN

Poem without a Category

The point in life is to know what's enough.
—GENSEI

With "my stick for companion"
as Gensei might say,
I roam these cold March hills
where a fringe of indomitable green
is forcing its way
through chain-sawed fields
and backhoed lots.
I walk the muddy ruts and think
how hundreds of years and half a globe
separate his life from my life:
seventeenth-century Kyoto,
twenty-first-century America—
what could be more different?

I picture his monk's hut,
its thatched, leaky roof,
high on Grass Hill above the "dusty world"
of coming and going.
Oh, Gensei, it's much dustier now,
our lives are so little,
our wants are so big.

I see his robed figure,
frail and bald,
afflicted by boils,
climbing through pines
and leafy bamboo,
ten thousand hollow stalks
of Buddha mind.
Gensei, I'm blown about by a damp wind
through thistle and broomweed,
it's all that I have;
my shadow on concrete
expands with your shadow,
fills with the shadows
of countless Buddhas.
I, too, "stand at the river brink
about to go home,"
if only I could find it.

I gather a supper of sparse greens
washed by yesterday's rain, imagine him
serving the "wisdom gruel" at the end
of his simple day:
studying scripture, writing poetry,
caring for his elderly parents.
"The point in life is to know what's enough"—
his words come back
as I smell the coriander,
as I turn toward the door, slowly,
in the fullness of twilight.

SUZANNE FREEMAN is an eldercare worker and writer who lives in the hill country of Texas, where she is an active non-participant in SUV/cell phone/dot-com culture. Her poetry has appeared in numerous publications, including *Borderlands: Texas Poetry Review, Green Fuse, Rattle, Southwestern American Literature,* and the anthology *Getting over the Color Green.*

PAUL GORDON

The Old Priest

AN OLD PRIEST, COMING CLOSE TO THE END OF HIS LIFE, still alone with his mysteries, his fingertips soiled with holy crumbs, one morning set down his reading glasses, looked up from his newspaper, and remembered the wide-eyed infant he'd held at baptism. He knew that it was no particular infant. It was all of them, uncountable by now, the many become one, weightless and frightened in the bend of his elbow, struggling to align its eyes on his face. The eyes, liquid and twinkling, are the only part of the body that never shows age.

He trembled. He held up his hands and looked at them for something familiar. He did not feel them throbbing with power. He watched the last thread of steam rise from his coffee and thought again of the infant. He moved his fingers slowly against the grinding of his arthritis, and, with a twinge of emptiness, he discovered a horrifying thing.

There had been no sin in that infant.

He saw something that frightened him even more. He looked into his own heart and saw there was no sin there either. And he knew there never had been. He came to the only reasonable conclusion to this musing. He realized that there was no sin anywhere. Misdeed, yes, and even evil, perhaps, but no sin, no fundamental wrongness, no essential offense in the sight of God.

He wound his aching fingers into a fist. Seeing how close he was to reducing himself to irrelevance, he sat perfectly still. He sat that way for a long time. The remains of his breakfast chilled in front of him. Elsewhere in the rectory, doors slammed, telephones chirped, radiators clanged. There was even music coming from a radio, deep thumping music from a car waiting out a red light in the street, but all the sounds felt distant, as if muffled by sleepiness, as if heard underwater.

Opposite:
Francisco José de Goya
The Repentant St. Peter.
Oil on canvas,
28¾×25¼ in.,
ca. 1820–1824.
The Phillips Collection,
Washington, D.C.
Acquired 1936.

In time a small voice spoke to him. He looked up into the quiet drafty morning that filled the rectory kitchen.

"Isn't sorrow enough? Do you really need sin too?"

The priest now saw the baby's eyes focused squarely on his own. "Yes," he said. "Of course we do."

"But you don't believe in sin anymore. You just discovered that."

"Doubt comes and then passes," he said. "It's God's test of our faith. What matters is that I still know better. Yes, we need sin. We have to understand our sorrow somehow. We have to know where it comes from. How can we do that unless we know that somehow we are responsible for it? Who can we blame if not ourselves?"

"Who indeed?" offered the infant.

"Yes, who but ourselves? How else are we to know our lives matter? Sin is the price we pay for our free will, for being conscious, for being human and not a pile of stones. Thousands of bacteria die every time I brush my teeth. Without sin, how can we be any more than they?"

"If we aren't," said the child, "how much greater our need for each other?"

The old priest huffed. He ground the heels of his hands into his eyes. Stars swam in his vision.

"Listen to me," the infant said. "I remember when you held your water above me like Abraham's dagger. If you hadn't held me, I would have fallen to the floor. If no one had fed me, I would have starved. If no one had bathed me, I would have rotted in my own filth. Abraham saw all these things when he looked down at his son. That is why he put away his knife. In all these thousands of times you've baptized me, I've tried to make you see what Abraham saw."

"I've done my best," the priest breathed. "I've tried to help. I've never wanted anything but that. I wanted to be a father hugging a child waking from a nightmare. When I held you, it was to stand between you and whatever is out there, between you and God, even, and tell you not to be afraid. My only sorrow is that I couldn't do it all. If I could face all your sufferings for you, even your death, I would. But I can't. All I could do was give you baptism. And I did that. That's what makes me a priest. If you take that from me, that power to wash away sin, then what will you leave me?"

"Much greater sadness than any you feel now," the child said. "But much greater work for your goodness. Tell people they don't need to be forgiven because they were never sinners. Tell them they don't need to be reconciled with God because they were never estranged. Tell them to look into the face of a baby and remember the innocence with which they all came into the world. Remind them that innocence and goodness are still at the core of their souls. Tell them that the dark thing lying at the center of their heart isn't sin but pain so that they will love rather than judge each other. Can you do that?"

"Should I?" the priest asked. "Without sin, nothing makes sense. Now when people ask me why death and suffering exist in the world, I can tell them. People will still go on suffering, but they feel better for knowing. Take away our original sin, and what can I tell them? That I just don't know?"

"Yes!" exclaimed the child. "Tell them you don't know. Tell them nobody knows. Who knows what will happen when you do that? Maybe you'll all see how terrified and angry you really are. Maybe you'll all shake your fists at God and demand that he explain himself. And when you get no answer, maybe you'll all hold each other and weep. Then maybe you'll see that you have all the more reason to love each other."

"But what about morality?" the priest asked. "How will people behave?"

"How do they behave now? How do they treat their neighbors now when they perceive sin and not pain in each other's hearts? You can keep your sin if you want it. But you know what I'm telling you is true. You've always known it."

The priest sipped his cold coffee. "Do you know that I am terrified of going to hell? I am. Dear God, I don't want that to happen. I want to please God. But a real part of me is convinced that I can't, no matter what I do. I'm as sure of my own damnation as I can be of anything. And, believe it or not, I know it isn't a bad thing to believe that. I try to pass on a little of that terror to everyone I preach to, to everyone I instruct, and yes, to everyone I baptize. I do that because I know any decent religion places impossible demands on people. I must believe in my salvation and work for it with all I possess, and yet I must never believe I've achieved it. I must know I am never free from sin. Yet, without belief in salvation, I have no faith. And God asks of us above all else that we have faith. So I must always be striving but beware of achieving. Our fundamentalist brethren believe everyone else is going to hell. We are sure we are going to hell ourselves. This makes us better. Can you understand any of this?"

"How many times have you wished you could wring God's neck?" asked the baby.

"Many," the priest admitted. "But I've always submitted. I always will. Even when God slams the door of heaven in my face, I'll praise him. I don't suppose you can understand that either."

"God doesn't ask this of you," the infant said sadly.

"Who does, then?"

"You see everything as if in a mirror. You see them all correctly, but you see them backwards. Look at them directly."

"I don't know what you're talking about."

"Yes, you do. That's how this began. You saw there was no sin. You had a vision that upset everything you knew, and now you want to drive it out of your soul. But you can't. It won't leave. It's true that we bring much suffering on ourselves. We are shortsighted. We seek our happiness in things that ultimately disappoint us. We cling to things that turn to smoke in our fingers. We desperately wish true those things that can never be true. But the deepest sorrows of life are beyond our own doing—death, illness, loss, misfortune, unfairness. It isn't our fault these things exist. We shouldn't blame ourselves for them. There never was an earthly paradise, free of death and suffering; that was lost to us through our misdeed. It may give us some sense of importance and meaning to think there was. But there was not. These core sufferings of life are like gravity. They just are."

The priest huffed.

"The universe serves its own purpose, not ours," the infant went on. "The proper functioning of the universe sometimes requires something painful and even tragic for me. Gravity makes my life burdensome. It can kill me if I fall from a tree, but it also makes the stars burn. A storm may destroy my home and flatten my crop, but without that storm, the whole would not be what it is and what it must be. All that went before the storm and made it what it was would have to be changed, and the consequences for the whole would be catastrophic. Even the death of my body is a part of this necessity. These things aren't the actions of an angry and petty God, punishing us for the sin of having become what we are. They're the work of a God so vast that even his apparent absence is a sign of love because it's love for a creation huge beyond our imagining. Now do you see?"

"No. You're asking too much. You ask too much for anyone. There's no difference between the God you're suggesting and no God at all. Or maybe it's worse than that. The God you talk about is too big, one that's spread so thin and diluted so much that it includes everything, so you can say nothing about it except that it is."

"Can't you still worship something unknown and unknowable? Doesn't its being unknowable make it all the more deserving of your worship?"

"Even something that may not be there? What am I to tell people? That we're doing nothing but shouting into the universe as if we're lost in a cave, and that nothing ever comes back to us but our echoes?"

"You were right in saying earlier that doubt is a gift."

"I said it was a test, not a gift. But sadly . . ." He rested his chin on his palms and pressed his fingers against his temples. "Sadly, there are many times when I look up into the sky at night and see nothing but . . . but nothing. Empty immensity. And I hear nothing in it but silence. Whenever someone builds a bigger telescope, the universe gets bigger, and I get smaller. God retreats a little farther from me. I'm getting old. My teeth are loose. I wake at night to empty my bladder and then stand at the toilet waiting for something to happen, like a mystic awaiting knowledge. I have never needed my faith more . . ." He lifted his face from his hands and looked at the child. "This is part of my job too. When people lose faith, I believe for them. When they can't pray, I do that for them too. And when they're too secure in their beliefs, I doubt for them, so they won't have to suffer it for themselves. I tell them not to be afraid, that God loves them, and maybe most will believe me for a while. They'll take my word for it because I'm a priest. I can hope so, anyway. I do that so they can live their lives like children tucked into bed on a cold night. They don't have to be afraid. I'm afraid for them. What would you have me do? Tell them the universe is really an empty cave? That at the end of life, we might just go out like an empty lamp?"

"Maybe you don't give them enough credit," said the infant. "If you can face this terror, why can't they? Maybe they're all as strong as you are and as good."

"You talk as if doubt and faith were the same."

"They are."

"I can't listen to you anymore," said the priest. "But I know that all of it has to stay, all I believe in, including the sin. You may not like it, but it tells us who we are and why things are as they are. It tells us that we matter and why we matter. Take that away, and what would we be?"

"Free?" The child offered.

"Lost!" the priest snapped.

The infant smiled. "No, not lost. I didn't come to frighten or harm you. I came to protect myself and to protect all innocents from the anger and hatred people reserve for themselves. I came to teach you that the fury you feel is sorrow turned inside out, that your sense of isolation from one another is your failure to see the common sorrow that makes you the same. I also came to show you the way out."

"Which is?" the priest asked irritably.

The child answered with a question. "What is God's essence?"

"Perfection, love, justice, wisdom . . ."

"Play," said the child. "The play of creating infinity for the sheer delight of it. And now, the game is Hide and Seek. If you find what you're looking for, the game is over. But if not . . ."

At that moment, a noise startled the old priest, and the infant was gone. In the kitchen a faucet was dripping, and the coffeemaker hissed and gurgled. The quartz clock snapped off seconds as if it had restarted after having stopped.

The old priest rose and stretched. He walked into the hallway, put on his lightweight jacket, and stepped out onto the rectory's broad front porch. A splendid spring morning wrapped itself around him. He breathed it in and held it inside for as long as he could, then let it out with a hum of delight. A young woman walked by, her tiny feet floating on the pavement like leaves on a pond. She pushed a round-faced baby in a stroller and hummed private music to herself.

As the priest looked at the baby, it looked back at him with its toothless smile. The priest waved, and as the mother went her way, he leaned against a porch pillar and covered his eyes with his palms. "One, two, three . . ." he began, breathing with each number to make himself count slowly. He uncovered his face when at last he was done. Brightness stung at his eyes as he squinted toward the street. The woman and her baby were gone. But the whole earth was seething with spring. Above him the atmosphere boiled, the moon kept vigil, the sun collapsed into itself and burned. Planets whirled together, stars scattered like sparks from a bonfire. Atoms hummed and galaxies exploded. There were so many places to start looking.

The old priest smiled. "Ready or not, here I come."

PAUL GORDON lives in a cabin on the side of Putney Mountain in Vermont, "as good a place to write as could be asked for," he says. He works as a cook at a residential school for children from troubled families. "I love working with the kids, and the schedule leaves my mornings free for writing."

RICHARD MOSKOWITZ

Housecalls
A Doctor's Spiritual Journey

OUR SPIRITUAL LIVES can be largely taken up with repetitive exercises like prayer, meditation, or ritual, which serve to maintain or reinforce what we already know or to give us faith in the experiences that redirected our lives or shaped our characters. These experiences, however, often come discontinuously as if unbidden; they can rapidly assimilate and transfigure all that has gone before and continue to ramify and reverberate throughout a lifetime. Such revelations, though blessed in their meaning and outcome, are often difficult to tolerate at the time. Yet, they are like direct *answers*, while the years in between may be regarded as longer intervals of consolidation, of diligent but often unconscious inner work, integrating the lessons learned.

As a young person, I felt no particular ambition or calling to heal the sick, and there has never been another physician in my family as far as I know. Studious and scholarly by nature, I could have found a home in an academic discipline like history or philosophy far more easily than in a worldy career such as the practice of medicine.

Why I chose a profession for which I had little inclination, ambition, or special aptitude and persevered in it suggests powerful unconscious motives at work. My grandfather's death from renal failure when I was six years old, with its accompanying signs and portents of mortality, turned my life upside down. One night, while lying in bed unable to sleep, my thoughts and fantasies culminated in a vision that I too was going to die and that nothing could save me from that fate. At my wits' end and desperate for solace, I ran into my parents' room. From my parents' reluctance to discuss it, I surmised that death was a mystery I would have to plumb by myself.

Frank Blackwell Mayer. *Independence (Squire Jack Porter)*. Oil on paperboard, 1858. Smithsonian American Art Museum. Bequest of Harriet Lane Johnston.

Another such moment of truth occurred while a student working as a summer trainee in biochemistry at a cancer research laboratory. I received a shocking wake-up call that nearly put an end to my medical career before it started. Deservedly famous for its state-of-the-art research facilities in genetics, the laboratory derived the bulk of its income from breeding and exporting pure strains of mice, rats, dogs, cats, monkeys, rabbits, and other species for biomedical experimentation all over the world. From the number of animals sacrificed in my own work and the regular quotas of my colleagues, to the vast quantities we supplied to others for similar purposes, I quickly grasped the enormity of this ghastly enterprise and of my own undeniable complicity in it. Since then, no quality or quantity of reasoning has ever persuaded me that human progress requires the systematic torture and killing of helpless creatures, or that valid standards of ethics or science could ever be built on such foundations.

Upon entering medical school, these misgivings only intensified with the years, such that I continued to doubt my vocation at every step. As in most charity hospitals, our indigent patients were routinely taken advantage of by house staff and medical students in exchange for their care and made to contribute unlimited quantities of blood daily for whatever tests any of us were even remotely curious about. I can still hear the low, mournful wail that met us each morning as the patients saw us coming with our implements down the hall. After days or weeks of experimentation on veins often weak or compromised to begin with, our last resort was the dreaded femoral puncture, which took only a few seconds but left both perpetrator and victim holding our breaths until the huge syringe was filled at last.

On the medical wards, we were chiefly responsible for admitting all lobar pneumonia patients, typically alcoholics from Skid Row, for whom a high fever, productive cough, pleuritic pain, or some equally serious ailment was the only ticket to a warm bed and regular food on cold winter nights. In most cases, the sputum was loaded with *Streptococcus pneumoniae,* an organism still readily curable with penicillin in those days; but before beginning the treatment, we were expected to inoculate the specimen into the peritoneal cavity of two mice, yielding the bacteria in pure culture when we sacrificed them two days later. Since the test was largely academic, I only pretended to do it, never raising the issue of animal testing but unwilling to inflict or witness the torture myself.

> On rare occasions when the beds were empty and the wards deserted, I could almost smell the faint but ineradicable miasma haunting the place, like the accumulated residuum of all diseases past and present.

One of my favorite assignments was night call on the maternity service, where the miracle of birth sometimes occurred in the wee hours before anybody had a chance to step in and do anything about it. Listening to the women in labor from my cot in the next room, I often reflected on the word "obstetrician," derived from the Latin *ob,* meaning "against" or "in the way of," and *stet,* literally "stand" or "standing," all too well suited to physicians trained to stand in the way of the birth process in order to appropriate and control it for purposes of their own.

It required years of inner work for me to realize that the culture of entitlement that gives physicians and medical students *carte blanche* to do as we see fit and compels our patients to obey and even thank us for it culminates in the actual propagation of disease, both indirectly, by spreading fear and doubt, and directly, through overuse of diagnostic and treatment procedures with obvious power to harm.

During my student years, a pediatrician renowned for his work in the field of infectious diseases succeeded in proving what many had long suspected, that the virus known as Hepatitis A is transmitted orally by ingestion of contaminated feces. This knowledge was gained by conducting dangerous experiments on individuals without their consent, namely, retarded children at a state school who could not speak for themselves and often lacked parents or guardians to speak for them.

By my last year, as matching day for internships came and went, I knew that I could not bring myself to practice medicine in the way I'd been trained. After taking my degree, I obtained a graduate fellowship in philosophy, mainly to clarify and even resolve the complicated dilemmas I had just witnessed and lived through. Well before I found words to articulate or concepts to explain it, I knew on a gut level that reducing diseases to abnormalities and using drugs and surgery to try to separate and ultimately remove them from the patient incurred serious ethical and practical risks that I could not accept on a routine basis.

Three years later, I tried again, serving a one-year internship at a large general hospital with three-month rotations in medicine and surgery, and two-month assignments in pediatrics, women's health, and emergency medicine. Our instructors were the attending physicians using the hospital to care for their private patients, on whose behalf we might be asked to provide an admission workup, insert an IV, assist in surgery, or whatever else they or the nurses might require. In addition, indigent patients referred from the ER and outpatient clinics, which we staffed and ran, were assigned to our care under the supervision of our preceptor for that service. In short, we used the old apprenticeship model, which grounded me splendidly in how medicine was actually practiced, allowed me to learn at my own pace, and left plenty of room for close personal relationships with preceptors, nurses, and patients alike.

> As in most hospitals, the bulk of our instruction came from the nurses, who basically ran the place but knew how to make it look as if they were following our orders instead of the other way around. If a patient came in the ER wheezing from, say, an allergic reaction, some version of the following dialogue would probably ensue:
>
> Nurse: Shall I get the Benadryl, doctor?
>
> Doctor: Yes, thank you . . .
>
> Nurse: How much, doctor, maybe 50 mg.?
>
> Doctor: That seems about right . . .

One memorable experience grew out of my friendship with a patient in his forties. In time we became friends, and he invited me to his home in the projects to meet his wife, savor her famous enchiladas, and stay the night. At about 2 AM, he woke me from a sound sleep with some urgency to ask if I'd see his aged father, who was complaining of severe chest pain in his home across the courtyard. As I entered his room, the old man was sitting up in bed, leaning forward with his hands clasped over his heart and a look of mortal terror in his eyes, a textbook picture of acute coronary occlusion.

Though equipped with only my black bag and reluctant to treat him at home, I dreaded even more having to subject him to the alien, military atmosphere of the ER and the Coronary Care Unit, where the risk of a serious complication suddenly seemed even greater. Less than ten minutes after a shot of morphine, he fell into a deep and peaceful sleep, and by morning he was feeling much better and resting comfortably. When I left for work, his wife told me that he had recovered from at least three such episodes in the past without any medical attention whatsoever, a tale that led me to wonder whether many other patients might not heal better at home, too.

After finishing my internship and obtaining my license, I began seeing patients in my home, in order to make my practice more open, informal, and based on consensus rather than authority. My method was simply to examine patients as noninvasively as I could, using only the simplest tools and as much direct participation as the situation allowed, making the diagnosis, to be sure, but leaving plenty of time and space for their own individuality and experience to suggest a regimen and plan of treatment more uniquely suited to them.

At this point, I was practicing what might be called "minimalist" medicine, giving liberal helpings of education and advice while doing as little as possible of a drastic nature, trying to guide people through the medical system without their being hurt too badly. But with so few procedures available that did no harm or that I could wholeheartedly support, apart from acute or emergency situations, I had little to offer my patients when their illnesses worsened.

IN APRIL 1969, another experience profoundly changed my life. Over eight months pregnant, with her labor due in a matter of weeks, a woman I knew very slightly called to ask if I'd help her with a home birth, a seemingly crackpot idea at the time, which none of the doctors she had seen would even listen to, let alone cooperate with. While keenly aware of my own insecurity without nurses, colleagues, or modern equipment, I eagerly grasped at the chance she was offering me: a way I could function as a physician without risking harm to people or telling them how to live.

When Dorothy went into labor, I arrived at her house expecting to perform a vaginal examination straight away, to see how the labor was progressing. I can't say if it was the candlelight or the Bach playing softly or simply the rapt expressions on the faces of her family and friends, but somehow I got the message that the exam was something I'd been taught I should do, not anything that she herself really needed or was asking for at that juncture. I decided that if anything went wrong, I could trust myself to learn whatever I needed to know at the time, and that the best thing I could do right then was just sit down, be quiet, and pay attention like everyone else.

I still don't know how Dorothy herself knew what she knew, having given birth to her first child under general anesthesia, but she taught me the whole course that day, pretty much without saying a word. When her son was born, both mother and child were bathed in a soft halo of light, like a Madonna of Raphael or Filippo Lippi, and we all saw it and stared at her and the baby and each other, as humans have undoubtedly done since the beginning of time. As if trying to give form and shape to the awe and reverence we all felt, her nine-year-old daughter announced she was taking the placenta to school, wrapped it in a plastic bag and stuffed it under her coat, like a conspirator carrying an oversized bomb.

However imperfect my attempts to live up to it, that first home birth showed me a way to function as a physician and healer that still works and makes sense for me. Even the most enlightened hospital has to make rules for people, to act on their behalf, as if it knows what is best for them and their babies, while as a midwife I was only a guest in Dorothy's home, undertaking to follow her rules. My job was thus no longer to do anything in particular or to tell her how to give birth, but simply to be there for her in whatever way seemed most useful at the time.

But the memory of that birth and all that it meant seemed at first no more than a private treasure, a model for self-transformation in some general sense. I had no inkling that anybody else would choose to give birth in this fashion. It wasn't until about a year later, while living in a cabin in the mountains, that I was suddenly inundated with calls for help from women planning home births, and soon I became as busy as I could be, attending forty or so births by the following spring and about a hundred and fifty in the three years I lived there, long enough to watch Dorothy's wacky idea catch on and spread like a prairie fire through the subculture.

Without an office, nurse, appointments, or even a telephone at first, I was totally available to my patients if they could find me, an arrangement that undoubtedly weeded out more than a few, but suited me quite well and resonated with the frontier spirit of the place and the already flourishing grapevine of the time. It worked both ways. On the one hand, prospective patients needed to be responsible for finding out where I was at all times and for mastering the rudiments of emergency childbirth in case I didn't make it. For my own part, I soon learned the advantages of dropping in on them whenever I came to town, noting that something fun or interesting was likely to happen when I got there, such as finding the woman already in labor or simply being treated like an honorary member of the family for a while, not to mention the reward of a hot meal, pleasant company, and a warm bed for the night.

In any case, I never missed a birth, lost a baby, or had to take anyone to the hospital in those days, a record that I can't explain and certainly never equalled in later years when I opened an office, hired nurses and receptionists, hospitalized people when I had to, and had my full share of complications like everyone else. Only in retrospect can I appreciate how fortunate and indeed in a state of grace I must have been, as if consumed by the vision that Dorothy had entrusted to me and prepared to do everything in my power to be worthy of that trust.

Between 1970 and 1982, I assisted at over six-hundred home births, and the model of the doctor–patient relationship that emerged from them is as relevant today in my office practice as it was then in the field. Through its gentle, family-centered atmosphere, home birth also left ample space for self-healing and helped me investigate subtler and less aggressive modes of treatment in my medical practice. With my background in biochemistry and pharmacology, I naturally gravitated to the study of botanical remedies, combed through herbals, learned to identify many local species, made infusions, poultices, ointments, and suppositories, and gradually began to try them on myself and my patients.

My chief mentor was an old German woman who had emigrated after the war, owned a popular health food store in town, and had a large and devoted following of young and old alike. Representing a broad cross-section of ailments, the customers she knew and trusted would follow her into the back room, where she used a pendulum both for diagnosis and to select appropriate vitamins, herbs, supplements, and homeopathic remedies. At times, she sent saliva samples to an even more aged colleague for some sort of esoteric laboratory reading in which she had confidence that various parasites, toxic wastes, and other pathological residues could be identified radionically.

Although many of her procedures seemed like hocus-pocus to me, she introduced me to the vast realm of esoteric phenomena that intuitively I knew existed but had never directly experienced. She was also one of the finest spiritual healers I have ever known. Several months after giving birth, one of my patients called late at night with severe abdominal pain that had developed with alarming suddenness after a long trip to her in-laws to show off the baby. The pelvic exam revealed a taut, bulging mass about the size of a tennis ball in the area of her right ovary that felt ready to burst, such that even I was anxious to take her to surgery without further delay.

As a last resort, she begged me to call the old woman, who reluctantly agreed to come. On entering the room, she knelt down to the left of the patient and began to pray, placing the fingers of her left hand over the cyst and allowing her right arm to dangle free by her side. In a minute or so, her whole body shook convulsively, and I could almost "see" a current of energy passing from her left hand across her body, down her right arm, and out through her free hand. Proceeding to the other side of the bed, she placed her right index and third fingers on the right side of the pubic bone, a "pressure point" for the ovary, and pressed it firmly, eliciting a loud shriek of pain from the woman that nearly levitated her out of bed but soon settled into a moan and then gradually subsided after about fifteen seconds.

As soon as she left, I examined my patient again and found that both the pain and the cyst had completely disappeared, and they never came back during the two years that I kept track of her before leaving the area. In all my years of practice, I have never witnessed another instant cure of serious organic pathology to rival this one, and it convinced me that healing is always possible, even when we least expect it or know what form it will take.

THESE DABBLINGS IN THE MEDICAL UNDERGROUND led me to homeopathy, my next great spiritual adventure. In 1974, thinking to give *Apis,* a remedy made from honeybee venom, to a patient who was hypersensitive to bee stings and failing to make any sense out of an old text I'd come across, I wrote to a homeopathic physician back East, asking if this would be an appropriate prescription. "Well, sonny boy," he replied in economical Vermontese, "you'd better come to our summer school!"

Neither the sleepy state college campus where the course was given nor the rumpled clothes and advanced age of the homeopaths who taught it augured well for the future of the profession. Most of the faculty were old or semi-retired, and very few earned their living from practicing what they were teaching us. It seemed as though the whole generation of active, successful, experienced practitioners who should have carried the principal teaching load were missing. No less upsetting was the fact that the course lasted only two weeks, after which we were simply turned loose to practice what we had learned on our patients. With no established schools or teaching hospitals to its name and few retail pharmacies to send patients to, American homeopathy seemed headed rapidly for oblivion.

Yet from the beginning of that course, I knew that homeopathy was just what I'd been looking for, and that I could happily devote the remainder of my professional life to studying and practicing it. Long before I had given or taken remedies or seen them work on anyone, it made sense to me as both a philosophy, a coherent body of thought whose basic assumptions ring true, and a detailed, systematic methodology that followed from them. Indeed, it taught me how to do what I was already doing, making a diagnosis but allowing the individuality of the patient to guide me to the most appropriate treatment. By reframing illness as the attempt of the organism to heal itself, homeopaths search for whatever is most unique about the signs and symptoms and choose a tiny dose of the one medicine that most closely matches them to assist the healing process that is already underway.

As to whether it works, I offer my entire subsequent career as evidence that it does, having used it more or less exclusively in general practice for close to three decades with never a cause for regret. Without needing to write prescriptions or refer patients for surgery except as a last resort, I have seen remedies work beautifully in every phase of pregnancy and childbirth, and in many other acute and threatening situations, as well as save life, ease the pain of death, and give dramatic, long-lasting relief in situations where conventional methods had failed or seemed totally inapplicable. Two examples come immediately to mind.

A twenty-year-old woman, pregnant for the first time, gave birth to a daughter after a prolonged and difficult expulsion. Though well-formed and weighing over eight pounds, the baby was covered with thick green meconium, took one gasp, and breathed no more. Suctioning the nose and mouth produced only more of the same sticky mess, and by the time I'd tried and failed to intubate or even visualize the trachea, she lay limp, pale, and motionless, with a heartbeat of 40 per minute, responding feebly to mouth-to-mouth resuscitation, but unable to breathe on her own. I put a tiny, dilute powder of *Arsenicum album* on her tongue, and she awoke with a jolt, crying and flailing, her heart beating vigorously at 140 per minute, her skin glowing pink with the flame of new life. The whole evolution took at most a few seconds. After a night in the hospital to be on the safe side, she went home the next morning with no further problems and no indication that anything untoward had happened.

A thirty-four-year-old registered nurse had suffered from endometriosis since her late teens. Already a veteran of four surgeries to remove large blood-filled cysts from her bladder and pelvic organs, as well as several courses of male hormones to suppress the condition, she came seeking only to restore her menstrual cycle, having long since abandoned any hope of childbearing. Although quite painful in the past, her periods had long since become scanty, "dead," and dark-brown as a result of so many operations and years of hormones and oral contraceptives. In the course of the treatment, her menstrual flow became fuller and richer, and within six months she was pregnant. I next saw her for a different ailment eight years later: she had had two healthy children after normal pregnancies and uncomplicated vaginal births, and had been well since.

I am deeply grateful that homeopathic remedies are available without prescription, and that the knowledge of how to use them is readily accessible to everyone with or without professional training.

Self-healing and self-care are fundamental and indeed inalienable elements of our experience, even a political and human right, which no government or medical bureaucracy can justly abridge or take away.

Since 1974, I have practiced homeopathy more or less exclusively and according to the classical method, using only one remedy at a time for the whole patient, and preferring the higher dilutions if I can see the remedy clearly. If I cannot help patients with remedies and conventional treatment seems indicated, I refer them to somebody else. If practiced conscientiously, the method poses minimal risk of harm and allows me to learn and grow at my own pace.

On the other hand, I do not believe and have never taught that it is the only way to heal people or the best way for everyone. Far from being a panacea for all ills, homeopathy has major limitations of its own, some of them inherent and others that will have to be judged in the light of a new bioenergetic science that is still in its infancy. I choose to practice it because it is the method best suited to my own particular evolution and style. Moreover, even when it is better understood, I doubt that it will ever become the dominant mode of scientific treatment for this or any other society. Indeed, if it did, I suspect that I would lose interest in it and begin to look elsewhere for employment. I suppose what I mean is that nobody knows all the answers, everyone has some of them, and there's nothing to be done but work together to discover our several truths wherever we find them and to celebrate beauty for its own sake.

After earning his B.A. at Harvard, his M.D. at New York University, and a graduate fellowship in philosophy at the University of Colorado, Dr. Moskowitz has practiced family medicine since 1967, specializing in homeopathic medicine since 1974, and has taught and lectured widely. In addition to two books, *Homeopathic Medicines for Pregnancy and Childbirth* (1992), and *Resonance: The Homeopathic Point of View* (2001), he has written numerous articles, including "Some Thoughts on the Malpractice Crisis," "Why I Became a Homeopath," "Plain Doctoring," "The Case against Immunizations," "Vaccination: A Sacrament of Modern Medicine," and "Innovation and Fundamentalism in Homeopathy." A student of George Vithoulkas in Greece and Rajan Sankaran in India, Dr. Moskowitz also served as board member and later as president of the National Center for Homeopathy. He lives and practices in the Boston area.

MARILYN KREYER

Expanding the Core

HISTORY IS SATURATED WITH CENTURIES' OLD BLOODSHED brought about by the insensitivity and ignorance of one culture toward another. There has always been a determined resistance to accept diverse pathways to God. I have experienced this within my own Christian church milieu. Repetitive worship practices and redundant sermons have undermined the anticipation of innovative thinking, of being stirred by "chutzpah," the nerve to be different. By being told to obey the static rules and believe only a predefined vision, for me, the magic was gone.

I worry that the Christian world is driven by a sense of megalomania. The American Christian church body seems unaware that it is only a small part of the global mix. It operates oblivious to the fact we exist in a world of many variations on one theme: mankind, the *wunderkind* of Adam.

Secretly, I began reading and learning about the Druids, Shtiks, Mayans, and other faiths. Avant-garde spirituality has never been welcome in the traditional Christian church, and mysticism is anathema. But I believe it is possible to appreciate the spiritual in nature without worshiping nature as God.

A profound difference exists between appreciating and worshiping. The practice of one need not necessarily jeopardize the other. I want to embrace past primitive generations and their notions of the relationship among sun, moon, stars, and their own lives. I want to learn the orderly movement of the stars without seeking the counseling of the zodiac. I want to appreciate the love in the hearts of people who dance in adoration of the earth, wind, and fire without applying for membership in their sect.

I have been taught if one accepts Jesus Christ as the Son of God and believes in the cross-work of his death and resurrection, all will be well. But I also want to incorporate pictures of Native American dances, admire Precambrian wall paintings of long-forgotten gods. I don't want to be made to feel guilty for enjoying today's New Age music with its harmonic consonance and nonlinear song forms. Surely, not everything in the secular life must be viewed as a threat to the sacred. My faith in the divinity of Jesus of Nazareth as the Son of God cannot be weakened by my enjoyment of Celtic monotonic chants or seeking the counsel of the Buddhist wisdom proverbs.

Because of my silence about exploring these new readings, there has been no pressure put on me to stifle my interest in the dynamics of other faiths. Undoubtedly, the expedient conduct would be to retreat into my Christian shell and keep my mind focused on the need to constantly repent for my own shortcomings.

Yet how can I? How can I turn away from all there is to admire of God's kaleidoscope world? Can all that variability be only evil? Is it not of his doing? I honestly don't believe "human secularism" is that inventive. I know the devil is clever and beautiful, but am I not allowed to enjoy beauty in and for itself? Why should "they" deny me the right to hug a tree, anoint myself in the ocean, or even carve my own totem pole? I long to hear the rhythms of strange faiths and feel the joy in uniting with foreign hearts.

God did not create me a mindless robot. I believe I am obligated to use my divinely endowed free will to better discern God and honor all he has done. And if I maintain theological vigilance, why not allow myself to enjoy the unique, the fanciful, and the sincere notions that exist beyond the traditional Christian worldview. In so doing, I feel certain I will find an even more magnificent God within the diversity of his creations. Surely there is no finer way to appreciate him than to recognize his work—all of it.

So the questions remain: Do I dare go down this different path? Do I have the right? How many dimensions are there to God? Is heaven really populated only by Christians? Everything in me says my examining quest is a good thing, and it is my dream that perhaps one fine day God and I will sit down over coffee, and because of my seeking we'll have so much more to talk about.

MARILYN KREYER's devotions have been published with the Baptists, Presbyterians, Catholics, and Evangelicals. She is now turning her attention to writing essays.

Opposite:
Kurt Schwitters.
Radiating World (Merzbild 31B).
Oil and paper collage on cardboard, 37½×26¾ in., 1920.
The Phillips Collection, Washington, D.C.
Gift of the estate of Katherine S. Dreier, 1953.

WESLEY MCNAIR

Pondside (for Diane)

The canoe shadow
by the still
canoe bends
and wiggles

and straightens.
Fifty feet out
from the camp
on the far shore,

a brown boat
with a green
cabin floats
among

inverted birches.
Where does it
come from,
this growing

island of waves,
this wind
within windlessness?
In the feathery,

exact reflection
of a spruce
surrounded by
a twilight sky,

one circle,
then a second opens
to the under
world.

WESLEY MCNAIR has received fellowships from the Rockefeller, Fulbright, and Guggenheim Foundations. Featured on Garrison Keillor's *Writer's Almanac,* his work has appeared in the *Pushcart Prize Annual, The Best American Poetry,* and over fifty anthologies and textbooks. Author of seven collections of poetry, his most recent is *Fire* (Godine, 2002). His essays about poetry in New England, *Mapping the Heart: Reflections on Place and Poetry,* were published by Carnegie Mellon (2003).

BARBI SCHULICK

The Awakening

I WAS A TEACHER OF TRANSCENDENTAL MEDITATION (TM) and a follower of a white-robed Indian named Maharishi Mahesh Yogi. Thirty years later, I can still recall the feeling I had when I was around him—a feeling as if angels were playing with the ends of my hair and surrounding me with golden light.

Was it the fasting? The countless hours of meditation? Was I mildly psychotic from the rigors of his retreats? Or could it be that Maharishi was actually something special, and when he walked into a room, it was with an entourage of heavenly hosts that some of us caught a glimpse of now and then?

I haven't yet figured that out, and though I am grateful to Maharishi for instilling me with the passion and discipline to pursue a lifetime of spiritual practice, I eventually chose not to be his devotee, or in TM argot, one of his "Knowers of Reality." When under his tutelage, however, I was prone to seeing all things as One—the flower in Maharishi's hand melting into his touch, the bottom of a vase joyously merging with a tabletop—I now think of my years spreading his teachings with more chagrin than joy. I sometimes feel like apologizing to the devout Catholics and Jews whom I assured TM wasn't a religion and whom I then led to bow down to a picture of Maharishi's master during their instruction. I find it hard to believe I promised enlightenment in five to eight years to all those who meditated twice daily and communicated the assumption, no, the conviction that I was among the chosen few who could deliver our broken world into Maharishi's Age of Enlightenment.

I condescended to all other paths because, as Maharishi put it, TM was the jet plane of spiritual practices, and, therefore, the "Zenies," Hatha Yogis, Sufis, etc., were only in helicopters or trains. They might get "there," but more slowly and with more bumps along the way. And though I had traveled via several of these "trains" myself, I now thought of my induction into the TM community as the most precious of all spiritual rites. This is what I had always been seeking—through the disillusioned years of Hebrew school and inside every spiritual book that found its way into my eager hands: Hesse's *Siddhartha*, Salinger's *Franny and Zooey*, Ram Dass' *Be Here Now*. They were all leading me to Maharishi.

Clothed in conservative dresses and low-heeled pumps, I gave introductory lectures and whispered mantras into my students' ears. I looked like a born-again bankteller. Maharishi made sure no saris or coral beads revealed our hidden passions. I spoke with words only barely my own. I was a coed version of a sixty-year-old monk. My sentences ended with a Hindi lilt, erasing traces of my New York Jewish roots, erasing any trace of me.

My mother told me I lost my sense of humor during those years. My jeans lay forgotten in my closet; my college friends stopped calling lest I try to convert them again. All my friends were now TM teachers who dressed and thought like me. The TM movement was my church, my school, my political party. I chose a husband I was certain Maharishi would approve of; I sent my first child to TM daycare. I signed off of phone calls with the prescribed "Jai Guru Dev," as habitually as if it were "So long" or "Take care." Most fantastic: I believed that I could levitate, or even fly.

At a point well into my TM career, I traveled to Switzerland to receive levitation instruction. I try to conjure up what was going through my head en route to this course. Did I really believe I could be taught to defy gravity? Did I believe anyone could? Yes and no. Yes because I'd read *Autobiography of a Yogi*, which convincingly described yogis performing such feats, and, most importantly, because Maharishi said we could. And no, because, well, that should be obvious.

Within a week, I was sitting in the lotus position and hopping around on a foam mattress like a frog. But a very happy frog, indeed. A spark of bliss would alight at the base of my spine and travel upwards, igniting each vertebra like a pin ball, gathering points until it lit up my skull, and Pow!, I was off, hopping across a foam expanse. Up and down we all hopped, like yogic pogo sticks, digging our knees into foam, flinging forward, and flopping down on our bottoms, until we were off again.

It felt good. Very good. There was no harm in that. The harm came later when I arrived home with a foam mattress roped onto the top of my car and spent every evening depleting my parents' patience while quaking the floors of their suburban home. But my pounding was not the worst of it. It was the wash of ecstasy on my face when I finally came down to supper that really unnerved them—along with

Opposite: Kenneth Keith Forbes. *The Yellow Scarf.* Oil on canvas. 61.3×51.1 cm., 1924. Art Gallery of Ontario, Toronto. Gift of the Canadian National Exhibition Association, 1965.

the smug certainty that someday they'd see I was right because someday I'd move past hopping into full-blown hovering. I'd hover cross-legged, inches above the dinner table, careful not to dip a knee into the gravy, and my parents would gaze upward, mouths open, in awe of their daughter, their Knower of Reality.

But as years rolled on, my reality did not evolve into the one Maharishi had predicted. Complexities of adult life, such as a dying father and colicky baby, moved me to question my master and his magic. And, to compound matters, I started noticing that some of the people I had once dismissed as less-evolved "non-meditators," or followers of "inferior" paths, were actually far more balanced and in control of their lives than many of my TM teacher-friends and I were. Still, when an opportunity arose to boost my meditation practice with yet another of Maharishi's advanced techniques, I showed up—but this time with only half a heart and a hard-to-write check for $450.

I waited, with a group of practitioners, for three hours in the halls of an upscale Boston hotel where the technique was to be given. Our initiation flowers drooped and our offering bananas browned until we were finally led throughout the hotel and into the incense-filled initiation room. As the ceremony began, I sang along with the Sanskrit chant, and felt, as I always had, a wave of peace from those ancient words. When I received my advanced mantra, I was in fact awakened, though not to the power of the mantra. Having just been traipsed through a busy hotel restaurant in my stocking feet, holding daisies, a pear, and a banana after waiting all afternoon and spending a month's rent for a meaningless sound, I was awakened to a state of humiliation.

My thoughts flew to my husband who had wisely refused to attend and who had months earlier grown a "forbidden" beard, for which our TM friends had given him a hard time. These were the same friends who had failed to comfort me at the loss of my father by assuring me he would be reborn into a family of yogis, simply because he had been a meditator. I looked around me at all the unnaturally glowing faces and wondered: am I a member of a cult?

I've never been quite sure. That day, I left the hotel quickly, locating my pumps among dozens like them in the hallway. When I got home, I threw them off, dug out my jeans and an old tie-dyed T-shirt and poured my body into them. Then, I looked in the mirror and very slowly began to recognize myself again.

I saw the seeker I'd always been—starting at six when I stood blissfully knee deep in autumn leaves and gazed up at a glorious blue sky. And again at fifteen, when uninspired by religious services I challenged my rabbi to define God and came away unconvinced of his experience. And at nineteen, on the day of my TM instruction, when bliss again resonated and cleared the foggy layers of my consciousness, filling the halls of the meditation center with silence.

Now I marveled at my thirty-year-old reflection in the mirror, wearing jeans for the first time in ten years. I picked up one of my discarded pumps on the floor and reflected on Maharishi with a confusing mix of gratitude and resentment. Could I blame the master for the trappings of his movement? I didn't know, but I did know I could no longer represent his cause.

I moved on—nursing an amalgamation of emotions, vowing never to follow a guru again. Yet I felt like an infidel as I experimented with alternative meditation forms and shipped off my levitation practice to the yogis of the Himalayas. But, in time, my guilt was assuaged, and I remembered that Maharishi didn't hold a monopoly on the spiritual. There were angels assigned to other posts waiting to be revealed. I found them inside the beat of a Kabalistic chant, leaping off the pages of a Buddhist bestseller, and trickling up my spine as I swung into a yogic shoulder stand.

The spiritual, I know now, has been hidden in every moment of my fifty years, be they confused or certain, angry or benign. And on those mornings when I close my eyes to meditate and the clouds clear, it may visit me still—though I long ago parted with my TM mantra and a special little man, encased in gold light.

BARBI SCHULICK writes, cares for her family, and tutors high-school students in southeastern Vermont. Her work has aired regularly on National Public Radio affiliate, WFCR, in Amherst, Massachusetts, and been published in *Yoga Journal, A Real Life,* and *Inside.* She is also co-founder of the herbal business New Chapter, Inc.

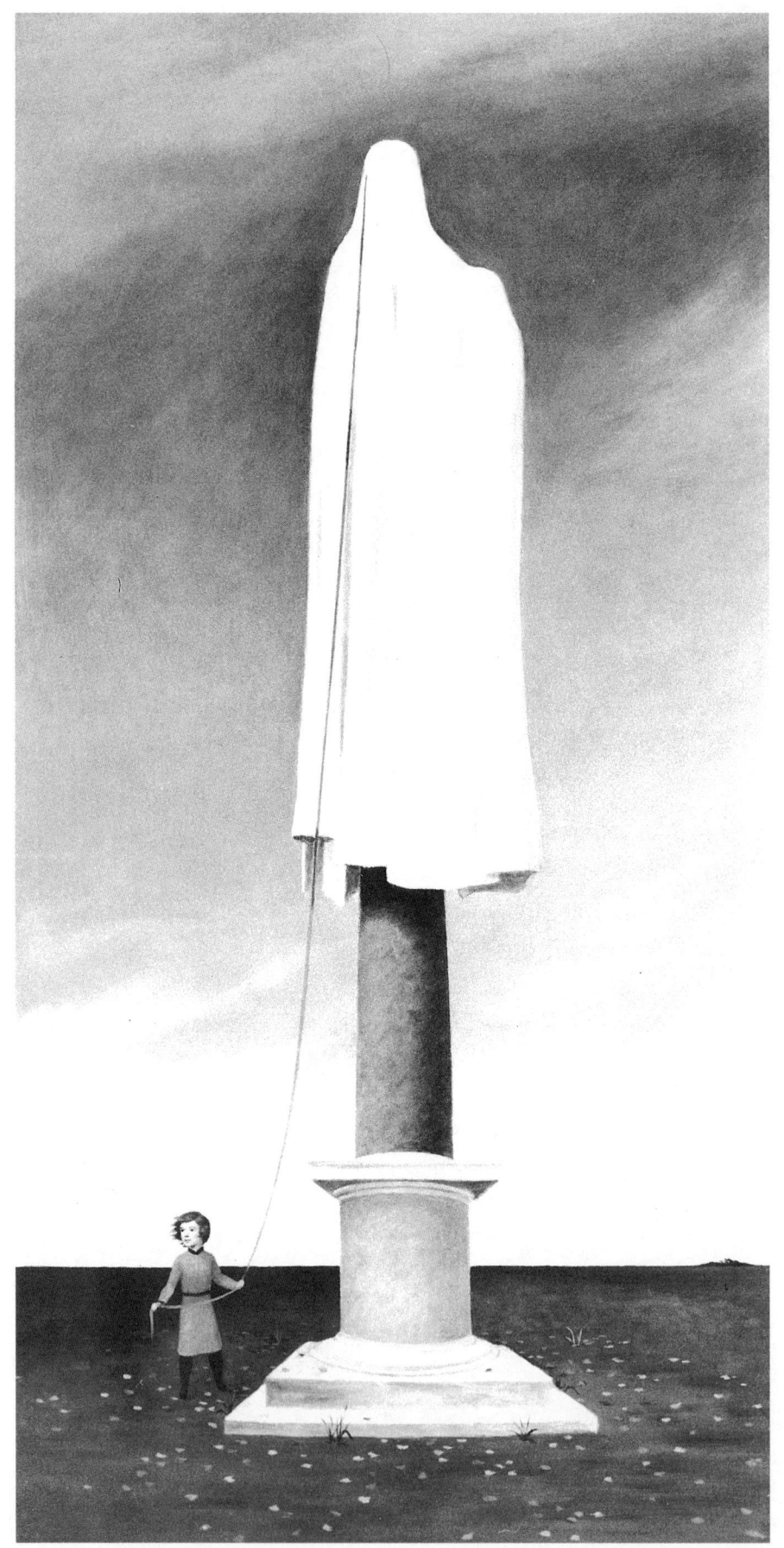

DOROTHEA HARVEY

Reinventing Your Life's Mythology

ONE DAY IN MY CAR A FEW YEARS AGO, it came over me—probably in the region of my heart—*the guiding myth that had been my strength in life was the Amazon.* In Greek mythology she was the warrior. She was strong. Despite all handicaps, she would conquer. In fact, to use the bow effectively, she cut off a breast, sacrificing the very symbol of her womanhood.

The Amazon had been my professional direction: I went to school, I joined the Navy, I went to graduate school, I started teaching right away—boom, boom, boom, and boom—with no time to think about what I was feeling or that I was a woman or about getting married or anything like that. But, at sixty-eight, I realized that living out the Amazon myth was not something that I wanted anymore. The Amazon myth by itself had become inadequate, unrealistic, perhaps negative. I needed a more balanced personal myth, one that would combine the positives of the Amazon warrior with the power of feelings. When I did this inner work, I made a very strange discovery. I found that my inner self was a girl. I never knew that. I lived my whole life as a professional, a neuter. I preached. I did my church work.

Part of this restructuring of my personal mythology meant taking care of that little girl, doing some re-parenting work with her. Every morning I took her in my arms, sat down with her, and told her that I loved her, that it's good she's here, that she belongs. All of this self-nurturing is easier said than done. When I first sat down and

Opposite:
Philip C. Curtis.
The Unveiling.
Oil on panel, 48×24 in., 1979. The University of Arizona Museum of Art, Tucson. Gift of the Philip C. Curtis Trust.

tried to say to her, *I'm glad you're a little girl,* what instead came out from my inner depths was, *Better you were dead.*

Eventually I learned that, as a child, I came to believe that *it's not good to be a girl. There's something very wrong about being a girl.* This feeling came from my mother. She was a child of an alcoholic and found that she had to put away her own childlikeness. My experience as a girl infant was: *If I let myself enjoy that closeness and that joy, my whole world, my support, will go away!* I experienced this withdrawing of my mother and concluded that I must be something awful because what I did was send her away, and, therefore, I'm never going to feel—and I'm certainly not going to be a little girl! I grew up with a resolute dedication to do for myself. I was always alone when I played, turning away from home, looking out for myself.

Although I got in touch with the little girl inside me, she could not give me the joy in who I am. Perhaps it was because my mother was simply not there for me at a deep, emotional level. Sure, she loved me. She cared for me. She supported me. She was proud of what I accomplished. She gave me everything she could, absolutely. But she wasn't there for me with any kind of intensity, that kind of emotional closeness. She didn't know that, of course, and I didn't know that either.

One important thing about this reconstruction process is that no one in particular causes the problem purposely. It was not that I scared my mother away or that I did something so awful. Likewise, my mother's withdrawal was a natural outcome of her childhood experiences. Growing up with an alcoholic father, she learned to protect herself. Don't talk; don't trust; don't feel. That's the way she survived.

I NO LONGER HAD TO LIVE THE AMAZON. My little kid already had approval. My little kid was created gorgeous, in the image of God. She is she, and it's okay that she's she. She doesn't have to run around and do things to gain approval. But to get that approval to come through, from my head into my heart, is something else. One thing that helped me was to imagine my positive, beautiful child and to think about what caused her to act in ways that no longer worked for me.

I believe that every human being, down deep, has that image of the positive self, that we, thank God, cannot destroy. We can shut down. We can postpone. We can bury. But we cannot destroy.

To rediscover that positive self, sometimes we must relive our earliest memories. Personally, I had to return my heart and mind to the first few times that I had a bath in my mother's hands before she got scared and closed off. I really had to push back to find this. I went back in time to a pleasant moment of my childhood, looked at the world from the height of a child, revisited the time of my very first joy-filled memory.

When you relive this past moment, look at who was with you; feel his or her touch; smell any good smells that were around you. Sense how right it was for you to be alive. Be fully present in this early child experience. Focus on the most pleasant, peaceful feelings in that scene. Direct your breathing into them, allowing them to intensify and fill your body. Every cell will come to life as these positive feelings invigorate you from head to toe. Feelings become deliciously vivid as they continue to build. You will remember those feelings because they are a part of you. They are who you are.

When I went back to identify that first joy-filled memory, I felt myself resting back on my mother's wonderful, great, big hands holding me. I could feel the love and joy in those hands. Knowing that security, expecting that wonderful, joyful, loving touch, smelling it, feeling the warmth, our worlds at that point were right, good, shared, and positive. Nothing had to be closed off. I could feel my feelings as they were.

Then came the change, when I couldn't be me, when I needed some protection. I needed to take on some kind of myth, something in order to survive against something—enter my Amazon.

ONE WAY TO WORK WITH THIS RECONSTRUCTION PROCESS is to describe it as a fairy tale. The first part of the story explains what happened to set up the negative myth that was no longer functional. The second installment tells how you want it to change.

Once there was a little girl who liked playing and splashing in the water with her mother right there. She was supported and loved. She could sing and play in soapsuds, feel the warm water, and say exactly how she felt because it all felt good to both of them.

But then the mother got scared and ran away. She said, *Don't ever say what you feel and don't ever feel angry, because if you do, I'll never come back.* So the little girl stopped telling people how she felt. She stopped feeling angry. She decided not to talk to anybody and not to feel at all so that this would never happen again.

The little girl went away to play and do things by herself. She sat under a tree, and she felt the line between herself and other people. She picked up that line and turned it into a sword, so she could keep everybody at a distance and have her own protected, special place.

That was my protection. I was not going to let anybody know what I needed, that I wanted help, or that I needed to be close. I was not going to feel and let anybody know my feelings. I was in control. This was my defense, my Amazon.

How did this philosophy of life function for me? After all, I took it on to survive. When I got to talking to my Amazon, she said, *I kept you functioning. You can't just do anything you feel like doing. I kept your attention on what had to be done, to do it well, to feel good about yourself. I put your message about having to be first and to be strong in a good light. I protected you from all the contradictory feelings that confuse and hurt. I gave you a goal that you could reach to give you meaning. I was there when you needed me to make it through, to finish what you started. I gave you a sense of honor and drive.*

I remember playing high-school field hockey. I would come home with a great bruise on my leg with no awareness as to how I got it because I had been totally focused on what I was doing. I was wrapped up in the emergency mode, the discipline of the Amazon. I was surviving, and I was winning.

Fortunately, my Amazon chose for me a career of college teaching which was productive, useful, and helpful to people. It just did not deal with all of me. It was a perfectly intelligent, useful job that had to be done.

A critical step for me in the reconstruction of my personal myth was to think about the shift from survival to living. I wanted to keep the strength of the original myth, but add to it, so that I could be whole. It's not enough to just survive.

My Amazon says, *You ought to be able to handle what comes.* But feelings are not something that you control. All human beings are part of a whole, and all human beings need closeness—receiving and sharing. Total independence is not strength. It's only half real. Substantial strength is being able to experience closeness.

The Amazon for me was the cutting off of my child, the woman, and the feminine side for the sake of winning as the warrior and to not become distracted by the need for the child, the husband, and relationship. The Amazon sacrificed her own nature for a concept. It meant living life as if it were an emergency. There was no time for needs. Always in a state of war, I walked a tightrope, with the constant tension as to whether I would make it. That's okay for a short time; it's kind of fun. But it's not okay as a lifestyle or philosophy of life. As I became aware of the little girl within, I began to experience her feminine side and learned that she needed time, that she felt feelings, and that she had needs. It was then that my Amazon myth started breaking down.

Ask yourself what is your myth, your philosophy of life, that no longer works for you. Then ask what new experience, what new thing has come into the picture, that conflicts with that philosophy. How does your personal myth defend those times of uneasiness? When do you know that something needs to change?

The final task in my reconstruction process was the creation of a unifying myth. The new myth can't be something that says that everything you have done so far is hopeless and wrong. That isn't realistic. That first myth kept us alive and brought us to this point. There are things in it that are part of how we have coped, and it's who we are. The new myth needs to be more encompassing, more universal. The Amazon survived in absolute loneliness. I took up that loneliness as my sword and said, *All right. That's mine. Now I'm safe because I can keep everybody out there away, and I'm never, never going to get hurt again.* The transformation to my new myth had to unify my need for protection from others with my need for closeness.

Using fairy tales, I was able to reinvent my life's mythology. Fairy tales do not need to be absolute or literally realistic. I could begin as an infant and then be the one who walked away into the woods. The time sequence is like dreams where anything can happen. You can go off in a balloon; you can make rhythms with a lion; you can do whatever you need to do. That's the beauty of working with fairy tales. You can take the philosophy of life that you adopted to protect yourself, add to it, and make it into the fairy tale that is right for you.

In my fairy tale, my little girl went off into the forest with a sword. She liked the forest and liked being alone so that she could choose for herself which way she wanted to go. Nobody could get too close to scare her when she had her sword. But then she saw someone else, just sitting there, enjoying the forest too, a medicine woman who didn't look dangerous at all. The little girl looked at the medicine woman, and she didn't want to go away. She wanted to be there in the lap of the medicine woman who looked wise and good. She put down her sword, got into that wonderful big lap, and it felt good.

What I did literally, sometime later, was to get a jewelry maker to make me a small, gold feather, which I wear on a gold chain with good feeling. That actual, literal symbol has been important for me, touching a depth in me that continues to let my new sense of self become real.

DOROTHEA HARVEY, a graduate of Wellesley College, served in the USNR 1943–1946. After WWII, she studied at Union Theological Seminary (B.D.) and Columbia University (Ph.D.). Dorothea taught at Milwaukee Downer College and Lawrence University in Wisconsin, and then at Urbana University in Ohio as professor and chaplain (1968–1988). She was ordained in 1975 and taught at the Swedenborg School of Religion. She has published articles in her field—the Old Testament—and is the author of *The Holy Center,* a revision of John Worcester's book on Jewish sacrifices. This article is based on a talk given by Dorothea, which draws on the work of David Feinstein and Stanley Krippner as discussed in their study "Personal Mythology." Dorothea lives in Gloucester, Massachusetts.

LINDA LANCIONE MOYER

In Idleness

At this desert retreat, on a scorching afternoon,
I seek out the dark adobe room
with beveled mirrors, piano draped with beaded shawl.
I delve in glass-fronted bookshelves,
breathing the gassy tang of unlit kerosene,
then stretch out on the stiff couch and read
from writers I teethed on close to fifty years ago
Maugham, Mauriac, Graham Greene.
I read at random, the way

I once lay around my grandparents' house on summer days
paging the volumes of the *Wonder Book,*
rich with old engravings, delicate typeface
and, same as here, pressed clovers, dead spiders,
penciled notes inside back covers.
It feels as if I could stay like this forever,
no one calling me. Yet in the suspended time
I retrieve an old urge, a hunger
to make something that will last.

I go out to get my notebook from my room.
Along the path, in the still bright afternoon,
I pluck from fallen oak leaves
a curved strip of bark decayed into an intricate sieve
that makes me think of old Pomo baskets
    on my grandfather's desk
next to architects' blueprints, envelopes figured
    in carpenters' pencil.
Once he held the smallest of those vessels in his palm
and poured water from a tin pitcher into it.
He swore that basket was woven so tight

    not one drop would escape.

LINDA LANCIONE MOYER'S poems have appeared in *Atlanta Review, CrazyHorse, The MacGuffin, Madison Review, Pacific Review,* and *Poet Lore,* among other publications. She has recently published a chapbook, *This Short Season.* She lives in Berkeley, California.

PART II

Healing

*Divine providence works things out
so that evil and falsity promote balance,
comparison, and purification as means
to foster the union of what is good and true in others.
God's divine providence, thus,
is constantly working within us to unite in our hearts
what is true with what is good
and what is good with what is true.*

—EMANUEL SWEDENBORG
  Divine Providence (paragraph 21)

CAL KINNEAR

The Laughter of Wood

In a pixilated age
we built it, our earth.
Dug two feet down
our bunker, our beached hull,
mortised, scarfed, clenched
old barn timbers, boards, shakes
and an oil drum.
To ward weather out,
hoard laughter in.
Chimera, half house,
half fire-mouthed dragon.
We swarmed over it,
sank the heat of our work into it.
There it stood dark,
doored shadow, our
sweat-, our dream-house.
We went in,
lapped in burnt thyme heat.
And you: you
went in, and inner, and
through, through
heat to deeper earth.
The laughter of wood
is fire, springing right
through our roof
into the night sky.

CAL KINNEAR is a third-generation resident of Seattle who writes from a perch overlooking Puget Sound and the Olympic Mountains. He has been a teacher, bookseller, modern dancer, waiter, sailor, hiker, carpenter, grant writer, and development director for a social-service nonprofit and private middle school. His poems have been published in *Fine Madness, The Louisville Review, The Licking River Review, The Prose Poem: An International Journal, Crab Creek Review, Birmingham Poetry Review, Point No Point, The Temple, Burning Cloud*, and RE:AL.

WILSON VAN DUSEN

Good Body, Happy Man

The Uses of Life's Difficulties

WHEN I DEVELOPED CANCER, I resolved that, live or die, I would attempt to learn. That was more than six years ago, and I am still learning. At present, the cancer is in full remission. It has left a small lump under my chin, which my doctor would like to remove. I have politely declined to undergo this surgery. It is a friendly reminder for me to pay attention to my body and the messages it sends my way, signals to the self.

Self and Brother Body

BY "SELF" I MEAN OUR LIFE WITHIN. In this case, I continue to see self and one's body as interrelated and interdependent, yet separate. This separation also prepares us to go on as spiritual beings after the death of the body. This does not denigrate the body because I see it as brilliant in its own realm. This separation is strongly suggested by my actual experiences. During chemotherapy, I had swollen hands and feet, and a slight headache: my body was speaking, but what was it saying?

Our body gives us transitory and chronic symptoms. Both call out for our attention. Without this guidance from the body, we may well fail in its care and kill ourselves. The chronic symptoms—the messages we receive over and over—are the more important. They call out to the self to pay attention, for compassion. If we seek some pill for relief, very often the pill doesn't correct the real problem. It covers it over, and the underlying issues remain.

Opposite:
Thomas Eakins.
The Thinker: Portrait of Louis N. Kenton.
Oil on canvas,
82×42 in., 1900.
The Metropolitan
Museum of Art,
New York, New York.
Kennedy Fund, 1917.

When I reflected on cancer pain, when I listened to my body, to my amazement, I managed to turn the cancer off and cause a massive shrinking of the main cancer in one night. In the literature, I found one other person who followed the same procedure with the same result. Somehow the body speaks to us in symptoms, but it is an obscure language we often don't understand.

The body is not entirely a physical machine. Saints have lived on cabbage soup or nettles for years. Everything should have gone wrong if the body were a simple machine that just needed the right tending. Then a great insight came to me. The body is like a faithful dog. It is a different creature from us, but one who wants to be with us, to serve us. It gives out its whimpers, which we must try to interpret.

Like the faithful dog that can do without much food or rest, as long as we show our bodies our loving attention, the body ultimately really wants our compassion. And how can we easily do that? By simply being with it when it expresses its difficulty in symptoms—paying attention, noticing its difficulty. That's what symptoms cry out for. It is very like sitting up with a sick friend when you (the self) really don't know how to help. I am convinced many a mother has healed her child by loving care alone. Love is expressed, and this is more essential than medicine.

Now contrast this loving compassion for the body to the quick downing of even the right pill. The underlying message of this act is, *Quit bothering me. Shut up with your symptoms. I am busy.* This is the direct opposite of loving compassion.

The real puzzle can be the body's nearly constant (in old age) language of symptoms. Clearly it is talking, but saying what, to what end? Is it saying *fix me?* In part this is true. A painful cut responds to cleansing and bandaging until the body can heal it. But the deepest implication of symptom language is, *Be with me, notice me, care for me.* Repeatedly, I have discovered that intense awareness of pain will cause the pain to change, vary, and eventually float away. But why should this happen if it is simply a physical problem? Fundamentally, our faithful dog or body wants our compassion. This compassion is more central than any medicine and can substitute for medicine.

A deeper issue lies in chronic symptoms that turn up year after year. Such symptoms are very difficult to read directly. The Hindus aptly say the aspect of life we neglect eventually becomes a physical symptom. In part, we can look at the very function of the organ involved. If our heart is involved, it must involve our life, love, feeling, any of the strong emotions that are central to our life, etc. Emanuel Swedenborg's organ correspondences and the findings of psychosomatic medicine are suggestive, yet merely suggestive, a place to start in the process of dialoguing with the body.

The fundamental pattern of chronic symptoms is that these call us back to the most central aspect of our nature, which we don't yet fully use and understand. Chronic symptoms remind us of resources we aren't using. But direct reading of them is difficult. Patient attentive compassion to the body is enough in itself. One can thereby resolve a problem without ever consciously figuring it out—just as a mother can heal a sick child without knowing either the disease or its treatment. So I de-emphasize figuring out the symptom language, even though it is full of hints, and emphasize basic loving attention to our faithful body. Nevertheless, compassion for the body's situation can lead to understanding what it is revealing.

Discovering Our True Nature

I AM IN ACCORD WITH THE EASTERN ORTHODOX SAINTS who viewed both bodily symptoms and outer difficulties as from God. It is just a shift in focus. Both are God coming to present a lesson to you, for your personal benefit. In this equation, I include all of life's circumstances. A woman has four failed marriages. The lesson is something about relationships to men. The problem can be manmade or an act of God. It amounts to the same thing. There is no chance in this conception. All our difficulties are created for our edification.

We can have short-term problems (the faucet leaks) or chronic problems (a businessman fails in several enterprises). Short-term problems teach us a lesson we can grasp and use. Chronic problems are more revealing. They call out to us that there are some things we haven't fully grasped and solved yet. When dealing with bodily symptoms, chronic problems ask us to reflect on them. There is, however, a difference. Bodily problems speak of a lesson within ourselves. Other people are not really involved. Problems in the world, however, speak of a lesson with others and/or God. For the most part, problems in outer circumstances teach us about our relations with others and the world.

Compassion can play a role in difficulties between self and the world. Rather than fight with people and the world, it is far more productive to attempt compassion with others. Try to see how they feel. Learn about the wider world. Through compassion, join with and enjoy others within the world.

Eternal School Days

LIFE IS AN INTENSELY PERSONAL SCHOOLHOUSE with a unique curriculum personally set up for each of us. This idea is the direct opposite of a design to life that involves chance elements. From the outset, we are launched into this school with an inner nature or program

> My hat is off to the Designer! The design is far more intelligent, wise, and in deadly earnest than I would have thought possible. It has to be a Bold Designer behind this design.

to realize. All of the difficulties along the way are set to help us realize our nature. The lessons seem extraordinarily difficult at times, but in the long view of eternity, life itself is but a moment. Some learn and move from grade to grade and even graduate with honors. Others aren't promoted and fail and struggle. The very central purpose of these lessons is that we grow and expand into our full powers. The full powers of one person are not those of another. Temporary difficulties are like special assignments, a little catch-up learning. *You are weak in this lesson. Here, practice it.* Chronic, repeat problems, inward or outward, are major lessons. In a fundamental way, this whole process of design is to teach each of us about our real nature.

Although we obviously share the same world, we are also on diverse paths. Inwardly we are of different natures, with different paths with different lessons. The discovery of our nature hangs about and apparently never leaves us. Our choice is whether the course becomes long, difficult, and painful, or whether we decide to move through the school with joy and delight. The latter happens when we are paying attention, if we take the schooling seriously. Learn or be damned. The central lesson is to learn about our nature, since the wondrous power of God within is our most fundamental nature. Since the central lesson is also to return to God, our source. To understand and learn is life. To not learn is death, spiritual death.

It is good that most of us have a lifetime to work at discovering our natures. It is difficult at times to see the overall use in this schooling, but, given time, it more readily becomes apparent. In eternity, the design is utterly beautiful and all good, even for those who appear to fail the classes. What a wonder to see it all as wisely created to such a high end, that we may be participating in aspects of love and wisdom itself.

WILSON VAN DUSEN was born into a household of no religious practice. He fell into direct experiences of God even in infancy. On his own, he explored the mystical traditions of all the major religions and came to Swedenborg and faith rather late in life. Now retired, he is occupied in setting down what others might use in hundreds of articles and eleven books.

CATHERINE LAZERS BAUER

Thoughts on Growing Younger

It takes one a long time to become young.
—PABLO PICASSO

Gustave Courbet. *Fox in the Snow.* Oil on canvas, 33¾×50⁵⁄₁₆ in., 1860. Dallas Museum of Art. Foundation for the Arts Collection, Mrs. John B. O'Hara Fund.

NOT TO WORRY, PABLO. More and more people are exploring that opportunity. Recent statistics reveal that every month the world's population aged fifty-five-plus gains 1.2 million persons. In America, the sixty-five-and-over population will grow from one in eight today to one in six by 2020. In that year, the "oldest old," eighty-five and over, are expected to double to seven million.

City, state, national, and congressional committees on aging won't let us forget we're part of those burgeoning statistics. Senior centers, retirement organizations, and prime-time publications offer the latest advice on taxes, health care, medical insurance, and retirement housing.

As a septuagenarian, I'm eligible for the information, but something inside me rejects all that guff about old age and what to do if it strikes. I don't think my attitude is all that unique, and what's more, I don't think it's entirely a matter of wearing blinders or kidding myself. Attitude matters in matters of age. Kidding oneself is not all bad. Humor is a compensatory tempering of the dawn of consciousness. Making a joke of life's absurdities makes them bearable. What's more absurd than wrinkles, forgetfulness, and sensory deterioration when you know full well there's still marvelous stuff inside you haven't even tapped yet.

How refreshing to be who you are, doing your own thing in your own good time, and not minding one bit that someone is watching. It's what I told myself one day during my daily walk, when I slid down the slide at the playground without even a tag-along kid to make it "legit."

My granddaughter understands. Now there's a kid with savvy. When she comes, we give the swings, see-saw, and the slide a good workout. We talk to the animals and collect leaves, stones, and crooked sticks. After returning home, she wrote me, "Grandma, don't ever grow up." She needn't worry. I was grown up once, but fortunately, I outgrew that. It must have been just a stage I was going through.

My daughters, successful professionals themselves, remind me that now I have time to expand my horizons and explore my talents. I plan to give it a try. I signed up to teach writing classes at the elementary school just up the road. I know who'll end up teaching whom. Kids astound me. They're our greatest teachers if we let it happen.

We're constantly told age is no deterrent to accomplishing significant things. George Burns kept us laughing until the final curtain. Grandma Moses and Winston Churchill came into their own after sixty-five. Betty Freidan, past seventy-five, writes and lectures about "conscious aging." Julia Child, ten years older than Freidan, is still chopping, mixing, baking, and sipping wine. My best friend's mother, age ninety-two, is proud to volunteer each Thursday at her local senior center "to help the old folks."

"Keep busy" is the perpetual admonition. Eat well. Exercise. Keep mind and body alert. That's the magic key. Try aerobics. Ride a bicycle. Square dance. Swim.

Listen, when your 1976 Oldsmobile sputters and rattles, you don't take her out on the interstate and open her up with your foot to the floor. Glory be, the rat race is over. Enjoy! The work of the world is no longer your primary responsibility. The older I get, the more I question the American work ethic; the more I think Thoreau's advice is sound: "Throw away a whole day for a single expansion of air." Climb a tree. Dance on your lawn. Sit. Relax.

A Denver teacher asked her first-graders to imagine what life would be like at age one-hundred. A six-year-old sage said, "I think I will become humble and stay home a lot."

Here in the magnificent Rocky Mountains, I walk a lot and catch my breath when I come upon an elk or deer. It's a thrill that never wears thin. I have a fox that visits each day and even naps on my deck. My neighbor watered my plants when I was on vacation. "Your little fox came and peeked in the door," she said. "He smiled, I swear. Probably thought you were home again."

To be who you are, to really look as if for the very first time, to explore, to marvel at trifles, to enjoy the right-now laughter of a child or the rosy streaks across the sky, to think the eternal now instead of time—hey, that's like taking a hot bath after a week at a cottage without plumbing. It's also what being a second-time kid is all about, living with reverence and wonder.

The pain you thought you could never endure, the paradox that constantly hit you in the gut, ultimately fostered a rebirth and transformation, a peaceful acceptance of, an abiding love for, a childlike intimacy with all that is.

Ashley Montagu had it right. "The trick in life is to die young as late as possible." His idea must have caught hold; more and more people are perfecting the art.

CATHERINE BAUER has sold over six-hundred essays, articles, and stories to markets including *Christian Science Monitor, Spiritual Life, Bloomsbury Review, Modern Maturity,* and *The Writer.* Cosmic Concepts published her essay collection *One Day on Earth: A Third Eye View.* She taught writing through the University of Wisconsin Extension, Ohio State University, and the University of Colorado, Denver.

STEVEN J. MOSS

Silent Retreat

Unknown.
Pair of Dancers.
Earthenware,
white slip
with traces of pigment
over white slip, 11⅝ in.,
seventh century.
Yale University Art
Gallery. University
Purchase.

"I HAVEN'T SPOKEN TO HER IN TWENTY-TWO YEARS, and I don't intend to start now," my mother proclaimed, scrubbing at the already-clean counter to emphasize her point.

"But Mom, it's a silent retreat. You won't be talking to her. In fact, you'll be encouraged not to," I said to the back of her head. Her hair was still mostly black with only a few specks of gray.

"Yes, well, as long as she doesn't try talking to me. I'm not having any of that."

I'd made the mistake of telling my mother about a retreat I was going on with my Aunt Gen. Knowing of my interest in Buddhism, Gen had found a course for me to take at Spirit Rock, a local meditation center. She offered to pay the fee and, after we talked about it, asked if she could come along. I was delighted to spend time with my aunt, who'd taken up Spanish at sixty and tap dance lessons at sixty-five.

After I told my mother, she insisted on joining us. Not because of any interest in Buddhism, but to make sure her older sister didn't spend any more time with me than she did. Still, she wanted to make it clear that while she was going to the retreat, she would not be speaking to my aunt.

"Mom, why don't you talk to Gen?"

"Because of what she did to me." She turned to face me, her lips clamped shut.

I'd asked her before and knew I wasn't going to get any information. Once, after badgering her for more than a week, she'd told me her grudge had something to do with borrowed money. Gen told me that her husband Sam had lent my father a few hundred dollars, which he'd never repaid. She claimed it was no big deal and didn't know why my mother still made a fuss about it. But I knew Sam, a gruff, self-made man with a long memory. If money was involved, Sam would not have let my father or mother forget about it.

Since I'd initially agreed to go with Gen, I decided to drive with her. Mom said that was fine, but of course, she wouldn't think of being in the same vehicle as her sister. As Gen and I slid into Spirit Rock's parking lot, my mother slowly rolled in beside us.

"Hello, Sarah," Gen called out, as we got out of our respective cars.

"Hmmmm," my mother nodded and glared at me.

The meditation center was cool and cozy. A few dozen students were already inside, shoes off, sitting silently. Gen and I picked out some pillows and found a place to sit. My mother did the same but found a spot as far away from us as she could while still maintaining a clear line of sight.

The teacher rang the bell twice and instructed us on the day's activities: silent sitting, silent walking, silent eating. I looked across the hall at my mother, who was silently frowning.

The morning passed quickly, and in my meditation I lost track of my aunt and mother, and sometimes, for a few short moments, even myself. I was surprised when, at lunch, my mother placed herself at our table, directly across from Gen.

Each of them chewed their food fiercely, their eyes shooting needles across the table. Then, Gen stuck out her tongue at my mother.

"Oh, oh," I thought, "Here we go." I silently prayed that whatever happened wouldn't be too loud.

My mother straightened herself in her seat and carefully placed her fork next to her plate. Using her hands, she pulled her mouth up and down and pointed her eyes sideways while wiggling her ears.

Gen burst out laughing. My mother giggled. Both of them continued eating, flashing shy smiles the rest of the meal.

Later, during walking meditation, I saw them slowly and silently stepping, arm-in-arm. From a distance they looked like two graceful birds dancing together.

At the end of the retreat, as my aunt and I were putting away our pillows, my mother walked passed us without so much as a glance.

"Wasn't that a nice day, Sarah," Gen called after her.

"Hmmmmmmh," my mother responded, without turning her head. She kept on walking out of the center and into the parking lot.

"Mom, Mom," I called, as I ran after her. "I thought you and Gen made up."

"No," my mother bit off the words, "I'm still not talking to her."

"But what about lunch and walking with her?"

"That's not talking to her," she said, but for a second, I thought I saw the shadow of a sly smile skip across her lips. She got into her car and drove away.

To this day, my mother won't talk to her sister. But every month, long after I'd lost interest in meditation or Buddhism, my aunt and mother meet at Spirit Rock for a silent retreat. I know this only because my aunt told me. Mom has never mentioned it. And, for now at least, it seems best that I keep silent.

STEVEN J. MOSS is a freelance writer and community activist in the Potrero Hill neighborhood of San Francisco. He's a regular contributor to KQED Radio's Perspective series. His latest nonfiction piece, "Confessions of an Expert Witness," appeared in the March 2003 edition of *Legal Affairs*.

DONALD L. ROSE AND MICHAEL TAYLOR

Go Ahead and Take Your Medicine

A SEEMINGLY OUTLANDISH ASSERTION is made in a book by Emanuel Swedenborg. He says you are especially free when you are doing what you don't want to do. What you DON'T want! That seems to contradict a recurrent theme in his books—the theme of freedom and love.

Heaven according to Swedenborg is wonderfully free because you do what you really love to do. But if love in action is what heaven is all about, what's this talk about being free when you are doing what *don't* want to do?

Swedenborg is speaking of a deep level of freedom—when people dedicate and even compel themselves. He says it may be easier to understand if you think of someone "willing to suffer bodily pain for the sake of health."

As a child, for example, you probably got your share of splinters in your hands and knees. Your mother removed a splinter with a sewing needle or a pair of tweezers. You submitted the affected limb and wrinkled your face trying to look brave. Sometimes you probably managed not to make a sound as Mother probed to dislodge the splinter.

"AFTER YOU."

Or when you contracted a cold, the remedy was a big spoon of cod liver oil. The bitter medicine sat on the shelf, challenging you to pour some into a spoon and to ready yourself to swallow it.

One day those knees that used to attract splinters might need to be replaced with plastic and titanium. The doctors have something Mother never thought of—anaesthesia. The overall experience of recovering from knee surgery, however, has twinges of minor agony. Eventually you become an advocate and apostle,
urging other people to get their knees fixed, to voluntarily accept the pain.

There are times when we need to compel ourselves to speak the truth and do what's right. When we don't feel like doing so, determined effort comes into play. Implanted in that moment of effort is a "heavenly own." You take on an identity, something that truly is your own. You are saying, "I, yes I, choose to do this." You are saying, "I refuse to be governed by my habitual avoidance of pain. I refuse to be imprisoned by the yearning to take the line of least resistance."

Perhaps we see this in people who set off to jog some miles when part of them wants the comfort of inertia. Or in people who do their yoga exercises when the body demurs.

"SEE, LAD — NOTHING TO IT."

Swedenborg says that something is then "formed in the effort of the person's thought." Swedenborg adds wryly, "And if he does not maintain this effort by compelling himself, he certainly does not maintain it by not compelling himself."

We see that the freedom enjoyed by someone making that uncomfortable effort does not feel like freedom "while the person is engaged in this self-compulsion." Nevertheless, deep within oneself, there exists a persistent faintly glowing feeling of freedom.

DONALD L. ROSE *is a grandfather who edits a monthly journal of Swedenborg studies,* New-Church Life. MIKE TAYLOR *lives in San Francisco. His cartoons regularly appear in* Tricycle, Writers Chronicle, *and* Modern Haiku.

WYN COOPER

Culinary

The best way to cook mushrooms:
hot pan, splash of oil, pinch of salt.

The way the egg breaks so cleanly,
its parts giving way to its yoke.

Chop and mince, crush and puree,
day drifts to night on a sea of garlic.

If the beef stock is red, let it simmer,
don't wait for the feds to crack down.

When the wine arrives from the cellar,
greet it with joy—it will do the same.

Dice thrice, philander twice
and you will get your due.

Garland stove, Sub-Zero freezer—
you don't know the meaning of want.

WYN COOPER's newest collection, *Postcards from the Interior,* will appear this year. He has also published *Secret Address, The Way Back,* and *The Country of Here Below.* His poems have appeared recently in *Poetry, Orion, Vermont Magazine, Crazyhorse,* and many others. In June 2003, Gaff Music released *Forty Words for Fear,* a CD of songs and poems Cooper wrote and performed with the novelist Madison Smartt Bell. He has taught at Marlboro College and Bennington College, as well as at the Frost Place Festival of Poetry. He lives in Halifax, Vermont.

JEAN ARNOLD

Cooking as Meditation

WE APPROACH OUR DESTINATION along many paths and in different styles. I have followed a pragmatic path using the logic that, since my emotions and spirit are housed in this body, I had best take care of it. Even before coming to the conclusion that spiritual, physical, and emotional well-being support each other, one of my life's goals had been to learn to cook well. Especially after I changed my diet from heavy meat-eating to macrobiotics, cooking for myself became imperative. Our society is not geared towards ecologically sound eating nor choosing foods with respect to the season.

Macrobiotics translates as "big life" or looking at the complete picture of life. To follow a macrobiotic diet, you eat what grows locally, what is in season, and according to traditional nutrition patterns. More emphasis is placed on whole grains, vegetables, beans, and condiments to balance the acid and alkaline traits of foods. You pay attention to how you feel emotionally and physically. When I'm feeling spacy and ungrounded, it's a sure sign that I've eaten too many sweets. If I'm feeling stuck and uninspired, I've been eating the same thing too often. The emphasis is on balance and abiding by the laws of nature. If it's the middle of winter, your body does not need cooling summer fruits like watermelon. Likewise, in the middle of summer, you are not likely to crave a hearty, thick stew.

I knew I had a lot to learn since I grew up in the sixties and seventies: a time when food was increasingly imported from far off places with different climates. Advanced technology made perishable foods available year-round. This trend led away from eating seasonal foods.

To learn to cook macrobiotically, I lived and worked at a macrobiotic cooking school and healing center. Learning how to use food for healing, I joked that I learned how to not only cook food, but wear it. I spent over a week wearing a tofu plaster on my shaved-for-this-purpose head. Open to experimentation, I noticed that I began sleeping and feeling better. I was thirty-nine years old, had left a steady job as an educator, and was walking around with a pound of tofu on my head under a bandanna, never feeling better in my life. How bizarre! I was following my dream and for the first time in my life was actively pursuing a course of right livelihood.

To each person, *right livelihood* has a different meaning, thank goodness. How many macrobiotic cooks could the world support? In choosing a fulfilling profession in which we are helping others and harming no one, we find satisfaction.

Eventually, I sought employment as a cook where I would not have to compromise my dietary principles. Initially, I surfed the internet for vegetarian retreats, but realizing that Buddhists are vegetarian, I narrowed my search to Buddhist centers. I was in alignment with Buddhist thinking, having lived in East and Southeast Asia. It was not long before I was working at a Buddhist retreat center.

After cooking breakfast and lunch at the meditation center, I was free to go on long bike rides in the afternoon. In the evening, I could attend the dharma talks or retreat to the sauna. While I was cooking, things were great. Harvesting vegetables and herbs from the garden and cooking them was like a meditation. Cooking for groups varying in size from fifteen to fifty, I soon learned how to gauge proportions and cook for the participants' needs. After hearing the story of a retreatant who referred to his small room as "the gas chamber," I knew to avoid cooking beans as a general rule. When I cooked for Tibetan Buddhist retreats, I could not use what they called "black foods": onions, garlic, mushrooms, etc. I despaired for days, thinking it was impossible to cook with this restriction, but I managed.

Despite the challenges, I felt calm and peaceful while in the garden or cooking. When I put food in the ovens or on the stoves, I set timers out of habit, but I often would check a dish just seconds before the alarm went off. Cooking became instinctual, second nature. I knew it was right livelihood.

There has to be more to spiritual well-being than this, however. I have rarely felt so lonely as I did at this retreat center. One woman on our small staff took an immediate dislike to me. To this day, I do not know what happened to precipitate this feeling in her. It made for a most unsatisfying relationship. The staff was allowed to talk to each other but often didn't. Interesting people came to the retreats, but after the first evening the participants went into silence and

Opposite:
Hilaire-Germain-Edgar Degas. *Italian Woman.* Watercolor and pencil on paper, 8¼×4⅛ in., 1856–1857. The Metropolitan Museum of Art, The Walter H. and Leonore Annenberg Collection. Bequest of Walter H. Annenberg, 2002 (2003.20.5).

could not speak. What torture! I'm not the loquacious type, but after a few weeks I was having my most meaningful conversations with the barking dogs along my cycling route. My communication consisted of yelling at them to stop yipping and nipping at me.

One bright event each month was the book-club meeting in the small Washingtonian town that was within cycling distance of the retreat center. I enjoyed reading the chosen book and then attending the group, composed mostly of elderly women. During the first session I attended, my ears hurt. These women had strong, loud voices, and it seemed as if they were arguing. At the close of that first meeting, the librarian said, "You don't talk much, do you?" I figured this was my one and only chance to get a word in, and I told them as much. I further explained that I was living at a silent retreat center so, to me, the volume in that discussion group was thunderous. They welcomed me to their group and said they'd try to hold it down. This connection with others was very important and much needed.

During this time, I discovered that I was holding a lot of anger inside. Why didn't my colleague like me? Why was I so resentful of her? Despite my wonderful diet, engaging in my preferred job, having a good exercise regime, living in peaceful, nearly idyllic environs, I was still spiritually unsatisfied. I lacked a close support group and felt very isolated. I did seek out activities with a friend who lived several hours away, but it was a lonely time accentuated by the physical remoteness of the retreat center and the silence.

I find it odd and amusing that I spent months at the meditation center and did so little actual on-the-cushion meditation. It's hard to be a human "be"ing after decades of life as a human "do"ing. I found peace in cooking, but in little else. I discovered some things about myself, but hesitated to dive in. Even if the water looks murky, I now know I have to pass through that place to get to the bottom. The next time I do something drastic like finding a full-time job and settling down, I'll know that my life must include more frequent and deeper connections to people—not just to other people, but to my own spirit, as well.

JEAN ARNOLD is a lover of language, travel, and cooking. Besides having worked as a professional macrobiotic chef, she has taught English as a second language in Spain, the U.S., China, and Vietnam. She wrote a newspaper column on "A Year in Hanoi." Jean continues to experiment with new recipes in the kitchen and in life. She is currently hoping to find a full-time job and settle down in New Zealand.

ASHER PUCCIARELLO

I arise like a doe in the springtime,

early, unfolding legs at daybreak
above the warm nest
made by my breast and breathing.
But where is the fawn
for me to nose awake and up
past familiar stones
in walls I walk and walk alone along
but cannot read the purpose of.

The grouse is done drumming
his hollow thrumming on rotting logs.
He's been found
by a hen who grounds his
every wild nerve into seed
as the sun sings through
fog and budding saplings.

Why does the sky
send only its warmth
wandering to stand on thin legs
beside me
nuzzling my coat, my ribs,
prodding me into another day
that will not nurse.

ASHER PUCCIARELLO lives in Putney, Vermont. He is a psychotherapist and poet. He has begun to explore fiction writing in earnest and is currently working on a first novel.

ANDREW CAPONIGRO

Healing with the Breath of Life

God breathed the breath of life into man's nostrils and man became a living soul.
—GENESIS II: 7

THOUSANDS OF YEARS AGO, great Indian yogis and Chinese sages developed powerful systems of breath control, which they used to master fear, heal illness, and attain the state of enlightenment. These ancient sciences of breath are so remarkably transformative because they tap into the spiritual life-force that gives our breath its life-sustaining powers. Although linked with the process of breathing, the life-force should not be confused with our physical breath or the air we take into our lungs. Our breath is merely the vehicle through which the life-force manifests "out here" in the physical world. The Hindus call this life-force *prana;* the Chinese named it *chi.* The Hebrews called it *the breath of life.* Christians call it the *holy spirit.*

In their search for inner peace, the Eastern masters discovered that all experiences of pain and fear are directly controlled by the breath. The Eastern martial artists used this knowledge to develop sophisticated systems of breath control for cultivating the virtues of strength, courage, and one-pointedness of mind—so essential to being a warrior. Our breath not only controls all experiences of pain

Opposite:
Atttributed to the Berlin Painter. *Red-figured Amphora (detail of Kithara player).* Greek vase, Attic, 16⅜ in., early fifth century BC, said to be from Nola. The Metropolitan Museum of Art. Fletcher Fund, 1956 (56.171.38).

and fear, it also contains the most powerful healing energies in the universe. By mastering the forces that dwell in our breath, we can gain some unique and remarkable powers for healing ourselves. In the words of an eighth-century Taoist master-of-breath:

> At its best, [mastery of breath] can bring immortality; at the very least, it profits toward long life. If the body is sick, meditate on the breath to work on the illness, and the sickness will be healed promptly. When the mind wills the breath energy into the limbs, it works like magic.

The Breath Holds the Key to All Healing

AN OLD ADAGE SAYS: *The doctor sets the bone, but Mother Nature does the healing.* "Mother Nature," the intelligent force that heals our minds and bodies, is simply another name for *prana*—the *spiritual life-force* that dwells in our breath. Prana does more than ignite the spark of life, it is also the *inner wisdom* that knows how to grow our hair, digest our food, and heal our wounds and diseases without anyone telling it how. In fact, the pranic life-force is the only force in the world that can heal.

The spiritual life-force spontaneously heals all sorts of illnesses, injuries, and diseases without the aid of doctors, medicines, or "outside" help of any kind. At their best, all medicines and healing techniques serve in the same capacity as a splint does to a broken bone. They can facilitate the process of healing. In and of themselves, however, they can produce no actual healing. No one can heal a wound on a corpse, simply because: no breath = no life-force = no healing.

Breath, Fear, and Illness

BECAUSE BREATHING IS SO INTIMATELY LINKED with the life-force, our breath controls every physical, mental, and spiritual process that takes place within our being. Unaware that our breath has such remarkable powers, however, most of us unwittingly tend to use our breath to block our feelings of pain and fear. When we do this, we create resistances or "blocks" in our breathing that inhibit the flow of the life-force as it moves through our system. With time, the blocks we create in our breathing become deep-rooted habits that disrupt our feelings of wholeness and can give birth to a host of mental and physical problems.

The Eastern spiritual masters have always taught that breathing blocks are a major cause of illness. In the words of one Taoist master: *Where there is blockage or stagnation of breath, there will be disease.*

My own experiences in healing with the breath have repeatedly confirmed the truth of these ancient teachings. I've seen firsthand how breathing blocks can create a broad spectrum of physical and emotional problems, ranging from asthma and gastrointestinal disorders to manic-depressive behavior and psychotic breaks. However, the connection between breathing blocks and illness by no means ends here. I believe that *all* diseases of the mind and body are inseparably linked with the blocks in our breathing. This includes physical disorders ostensibly due to "external" factors, such as accidents, infections, and birth defects.

Fear is the link that connects our breathing blocks with all forms of human illness. Where there is disease or injury, there is always pain and fear, and all experiences of pain or fear are completely controlled by the breath. When we feel scared or hurt, for example, we instinctively tend to hold our breath in order to block the feelings of fear in our mind or the sensations of pain in our body. Whenever we do this, we invariably create stressful tensions throughout our system.

In most people, these tensions appear as a vague sense of worry in their minds and minor feelings of stress in various parts of the body. As breathing blocks grow stronger with time, these ill-defined feelings can gradually worsen and take the form of recognizable medical disorders. For example, once-vague feelings of mental uneasiness can eventually develop into serious emotional disorders such as feelings of chronic anxiety, depression, paranoia, and obsessive-compulsive behavior.

The corresponding state of anxious tension reflected in the tissues of the body is the cause of many more "physical" problems than most medical doctors currently suspect. I have found, for example, that most breathing disorders, such as asthma and emphysema, are primarily caused by the fear-ridden blocks in one's breathing. Although extenuating factors such as cigarette smoking, environmental pollutants, and allergies often play a significant role in the development of breathing disorders, in most cases, they are usually not the primary cause, but merely contributing factors.

Ironically, holding our breath to block or suppress feelings of fear does nothing to reduce the amount of fear in our system; it only reduces our *awareness* of that fear. The fear is not gone; it has only been pushed deeper inside where it turns into anxiety. The layers of fear that stay trapped in our system exacerbate all symptoms of illness. In some cases, they can even create entirely new symptoms, which have nothing to do with the original illness or injury itself.

The good news is that this blocking process can be reversed. Most symptoms of illness can be significantly reduced and often completely healed by using the breath to cleanse the layers of subconscious fear that are trapped in our system and to send "booster-shots" of healing prana to the specific parts of our mind and body that need to be healed.

Pranic Energy Healing

OVER THE YEARS, I have developed a mind–body therapy, which I call *Pranic Energy Healing* because it uses the pranic life-force to promote mental and physical healing. Pranic Energy Healing employs a combination of meditation, breathing, and gentle body-work techniques that enable me to release the fear-ridden blocks in a person's mind and body and transmit booster shots of healing prana to the diseased parts of his or her system. These same meditation and breathing techniques allow me to accurately "read" the state of my client's emotions, enabling me to discern the repressed emotions that are linked with specific physical problems.

One of the most powerful aspects of Pranic Energy Healing is that it enables me to use my breath to "vacuum" pain, fear, and tension from another person's system. As I work with my clients, they can actually feel waves of anxious energy and long-held tensions gently leaving their mind and body. Most people experience immediate improvement (sometimes full release) of chronic symptoms that have plagued them for years. I've repeatedly seen how using the breath to release layers of "trapped" fear from a person's system can bring about seemingly miraculous healings of chronic conditions—conditions that couldn't be alleviated by conventional forms of treatment.

One particularly dramatic healing occurred some years ago at one of my seminars when I was working with "Karen," a volunteer from the audience. Karen had been in constant pain for thirty-five years after her leg had been crushed in a childhood accident. The first thing I did was to teach her how to meditate on the movements of her breath. Then I set to work with my hands and breath to draw some of the pain and fear from her leg.

Within minutes, Karen began to relive the day of the accident. She remembered how scared she had been in the emergency room, and how both her father and the doctor had sternly ordered her to stifle her tears. She also realized that she had been repressing those feelings of terror for thirty-five years. That evening the pain in Karen's leg disappeared and never returned.

Breathing Blocks and Self-Conflict

THE HABIT OF SUPPRESSING OUR BREATH to block unwanted feelings produces feelings of self-conflict and self-doubt. Think of self-conflict as simply a form of fighting oneself—a kind of inner civil war that depletes our mental and physical resources. Whenever we hold our breath to block fearful emotions or feelings of pain, we create contradictory tensions throughout our system that weaken our natural defenses and increase our susceptibility to infectious diseases.

As the following case history illustrates, self-conflict not only depletes our inner resources, it also can cause harm to our body by making us clumsy and accident-prone. When "Ann" called to schedule a healing session, she told me that two years earlier she had fallen and fractured a number of bones in her ankle. Despite her doctors' best efforts, the ankle had stubbornly refused to heal. By the time she called me, Ann's ankle had developed an infection known as "tuberculosis of the bone," and she was scheduled for surgery in three weeks. Her doctors were going to scrape the bones in an effort to stop the infection—but they weren't very hopeful about the outcome. If the procedure proved unsuccessful, they would have to amputate her foot.

During our first session, I learned that Ann was harboring intense feelings of anger and fear toward her injured ankle. Her determination to "push-away" her fear and pain was so incredibly strong it seemed as if she had already mentally cut her foot off at the ankle. As I worked to lift some of the fear and tension that had accumulated over the past two years, the pain, swelling, and discoloration in her ankle gradually began to subside. By the end of our first session, Ann was able to walk much more comfortably. She was less afraid to put some weight on her ankle and was feeling much less angry and resentful toward her injured body. By the end of our second session, her ankle showed even greater signs of improvement.

Our third session took place just four days before Ann was scheduled to undergo surgery. That morning, she arrived at my office with the wonderful news that her doctor had canceled the operation because her ankle was healing normally. Her doctor said, "I don't know what you're doing that's different, but whatever it is, just keep on doing it."

Ann didn't dare tell him about the unconventional kind of work she'd been doing with me, but she knew that it had made the critical difference. When I thought she was ready to "hear" my full diagnosis of her condition, I said, "Can you see that it was only your anger and fear that kept your ankle from healing?"

"Yes."

"Well, here's something else for you to think about. I'll bet that you were feeling angry and scared at the very moment you broke your ankle. In fact, it was your anger and fear that really caused that accident."

Ann's eyes flashed at the memory. "You're right! It happened while I was moving furniture from my dead mother's apartment. I didn't want to be there, and I was feeling so mad at her that I swear she pushed me!"

Healing with the Breath

THE HEALING POWERS contained in the breath are not utopian myths or wishful figments of the imagination. They are very real, and they are also extremely practical. You do not have to be a gifted psychic or highly accomplished yogi in order to heal yourself with your breath. Anyone who studies the science of breath with discipline and regularity can learn to access the healing energies contained in the breath and direct them at will. Learning to heal or alleviate relatively minor problems, such as headaches, muscular tensions, chronic pain, and anxiety, is remarkably easy to do. The more serious or deep-rooted an illness, the greater one's mastery of breath must be to effect significant healing.

Pranic energy healing is an inborn talent in everyone but usually needs to be awakened. Since accomplished teachers of this art have been rare, most people who have learned how to heal with their breath have intuitively developed this gift on their own. Pranic energy healers tend to be more common in traditional societies. Some of the *curanderos* or folk healers of Brazil are known to use their breath in this way. The same is true of certain folk healers in India and China. Healers with this natural healing ability can appear anywhere. I once heard of an old woman in a small coal-mining town in Ohio who could use her breath to "blow the fire out of burns." As long as the injured person was immediately brought to her for treatment, the burns would heal rapidly—without pain and without blistering. This unusual ability was passed on to her granddaughter.

Even without the help of an accomplished teacher, anyone can begin to learn how to heal with the breath by studying breath-related practices such as Hatha Yoga, Tai Chi, and Chi Kung. These ancient spiritual disciplines embody effective techniques for enhancing the flow of prana or chi throughout the mind and body. The healing energies of the life-force can also be accessed by practicing any of the time-honored spiritual disciplines, such as meditation, chanting, prayer, and the repetition of divine names. Nevertheless, the simplest, fastest, and most direct way to access the healing energies contained in the breath is through a knowledgeable control of breathing techniques.

Meditation on the Breath

NO MATTER WHY WE WISH TO PRACTICE BREATHING TECHNIQUES—whether to master our fear, heal ourselves, or enter into communion with God—meditation on the breath is the first and most important technique to learn. This is because the meditative state of consciousness is the only state in which we can access the healing energies of the life-force and direct them where we will. Furthermore, the effectiveness of all other breathing techniques ultimately depends on the depth and the quality of our meditative state.

Meditation quiets our "everyday" mind and guides it into a fearless, calm, and detached state that is known as *witness consciousness.* It is only from within this detached state that we can "return" to the feelings of pain and fear we originally blocked and give them the special attention they need. Although our breathing blocks affect every thought, emotion, and cell in our physical body, we cannot detect them in our "everyday" state of mind because they become second nature. Meditation on the breath induces a state of meditative sensitivity and inner self-awareness that enable us to perceive these hidden blocks and study them in minute detail.

While in the meditation state, the first thing we notice are the surface distortions in our breathing patterns. These take the form of various tensions, slacknesses, erratic rhythms, and brief cessations in the movements of our breath. At deeper levels of meditative consciousness, we can actually perceive the underground streams of anxiety that we have created by suppressing our breath in fear. The same techniques that enable us to detect the blocks in our breathing also enable us to release those blocks and dry up the subconscious streams of anxiety. Releasing the blocks in our breathing also enhances the flow of prana to the parts of our mind and our body that were formerly blocked and deprived.

Great Fruits and Many Blessings

MEDITATION ON THE BREATH was the chief spiritual discipline that Buddha practiced to attain his state of enlightenment. It was also the single most important spiritual practice he later passed on to his followers. Two weeks before he died, Buddha called his monks together and announced that he would soon be leaving his physical body. If they had any last questions to ask him, this was the time to do it:

> One of the younger monks rose to his feet and respectfully asked: "Please tell me master, what have you gained from meditating on your breath?"
>
> Buddha answered, "I have gained nothing from meditating on my breath."

Breath of Life

Upon hearing these words, many of the monks in the assembly became visibly upset. One of the oldest monks then rose to his feet and protested, "But master! If you have gained nothing from meditating on your breath, why have you been telling me to practice breath-meditation these past twenty years?"

Buddha calmly replied, "What I said is true. I have gained nothing from meditating on my breath—but let me tell you what I have lost. I have lost my fear of sickness, I have lost my fear of old age, and I have lost my fear of death."

Buddha once said to his own son: "Always practice mindfulness of breathing. When that is maintained, it brings great fruits and many blessings." The "fruits and blessings" of which Buddha spoke are available to anyone willing to turn within and meditate on the subtle movements of his or her breath in a disciplined and knowledgeable way. The fruits and blessings that you personally gain from practicing breathing techniques will mostly depend on the strength of your commitment and the amount of quality time you spend in making this kind of knowledge your own. May the fruits and blessings that you accrue from your practices increase with each passing day.

ANDY CAPONIGRO is a former concert guitarist who has been healing people with the powers of the breath since the early seventies. Internationally known as "a master of breath," he conducts weekend workshops in which he teaches special mediation and breathing techniques that act directly to dissolve pain, fear, and tension from the mind and body. His private sessions and workshops have provided remarkably effective help for hundreds of people suffering from chronic illnesses and deep-rooted psychological problems. He is currently writing a book *The Miracle of the Breath: Mastering Fear, Healing Illness, and Entering into Communion with God*, which is dedicated to the memory of Emanuel Swedenborg, the first known master-of-breath in the history of Western civilization. For more information, Andy welcomes reader to contact him at acaponigro@aol.com.

PHILIP LISAGOR

R'uach Ha R'uach

That wind, that wind
Shakes my tipi, shakes my tipi,
And sings a song for me,
And sings a song for me.
—SONG OF THE GHOST DANCE RELIGION

The dead do not praise the lord,
their lips are sealed in silence.
But we shall praise the lord
now and forever.
—PSALM 115

I perch on a cliff's ledge,
balanced, overlooking
the still canyon entrance.

Springs flow down the San Juans
from distant snowy peaks.
Blossoms on mesa trees.

A Red-tailed Hawk streams up
on crisp air currents. Nearby
Kokopelli dances.

Rustling wind from the chasm
carries up frothing of
water falling down rocks.

Oh constant chatter, my
inner voice. But breathing
stills me to silent peace.

Air moving in and out,
my chest rises and falls
in concert with the wind.

I resonate with this
canyon. Wind, water, and
the hawk's cry are within.

Spirit, come in as breath,
go out as prayer, and
sing a song for me.

DR. PHILIP LISAGOR is a cardiothoracic surgeon, currently serving as chief of surgery at the Reno Veteran's Hospital and assistant dean of The University of Nevada School of Medicine. His contributions to medical literature have appeared in numerous journals. As background for this poem, the author says, "I thank the San Juan mountains of southern Colorado for a peaceful spring day, which came as a gift along a Mesa Verde hiking trail. Just as all mountains are alike, each range is also different and speaks in a diction prescribed by local features and the people who have lived and died there. *R'uach Ha R'uach* is a transliteration from Hebrew meaning, 'Spirit, the Spirit' or 'Breath, the breath.' In Hebrew, as in Sanskrit, the word for breath and the word for spirit are the same."

W.E. REINKA

Landfalls

VIEWED FROM THE RIM OF WILDCAT CANYON, the distant skyscrapers of San Francisco form a tiny Lego town. Once upon a time, a nearby city planned to annex Wildcat. Sewers were laid, an access road paved. After decades of flukes and second thoughts, the East Bay Regional Parks took possession of the undeveloped hideaway.

It remains a lonely place. No picnic tables, Frisbee meadows, or swimming holes lure day users. Wildcat has no public roads. People must walk in.

On my favorite walk, I sidestep the gate that keeps out cars and climb the crumbled old access road into the canyon. I feel like a character in a post-apocalyptic science-fiction novel. People have vanished from the earth, leaving nature to reclaim itself mote by mote. By minute degrees, anise and artichoke thistles corrode old asphalt.

Anonymous (formally attributed to Asher Durand).
The Hunter.
Oil on linen canvas, 22×30 in., 1846.
Collection of Arizona State University Art Museum.
1951.086.000.

Scotch broom and poison hemlock stretch a little farther into the roadway every year. Curbs have all but disappeared.

Geologic eras, like the forces that scooped out Wildcat Canyon, are measured in millennia. But shorter measures exist in Wildcat—scars from landfalls, for instance. Some are barely detectable with mature trees growing in their trenches. Younger landfalls are covered with grass or brush. Landfalls left behind by last winter's storms still show fresh brown scars.

About a mile in, crumbling asphalt gives way to a wide dirt trail. I hike around what I call Reptile Corner where my steps sometimes freeze gopher snakes or send alligator lizards scooting for safety. The path follows a terrace below the ridge but still high above Wildcat Creek. Occasionally, a coyote slinks across my path, stopping to smirk before going about its business. Every blue moon, I look into the triangular face of an alert red fox. It immediately darts for cover, and I track its bushy tail through the tall grass up the hillside. High overhead, Red-tailed Hawks fly vigilant circles while, closer to earth, funereal turkey vultures, their tiny red heads looking too small for their wingspans, hang suspended on thermals. Sometimes I duck as they swoop down toward perches in the madrone and black oak forest that crowds the creek below.

On weekends I'm a hiker, not a walker, the way some people call themselves runners, not joggers. I churn past my normal turnaround point and puff up a steep trail where moist shade yields wild cucumber, miner's lettuce, and other treats that exposed trails don't offer. On ambitious Sundays, I power-walk through another couple of miles to a pond where turtles sit on rocks in the sun.

But my weekday forays into Wildcat are introspective strolls, work breaks where I walk out resentments and talk things over with myself. Weekdays I turn around at a horse trough about two miles in. As I walk back, I reflect on the landfalls in my own life—the frightening transition away from the corporate world, the surgeon telling me I have cancer, the loss of a child.

Some of my personal landfalls have grown in. A few remain freshly scarred. As I start up the last big hill that leads back over the rim, I spot artichoke thistle hiding what was pavement last year.

Like nature, we reclaim ourselves mote by mote.

W.E. REINKA has published stories, essays, reviews, and articles in over eighty publications nationwide. He is a member of the Society of Children's Book Writers & Illustrators and the Mystery Writers of America. Formerly the contributing editor (Books) for the *Berkeley Insider* and *Berkeley Voice,* he and his family recently moved to Eugene, Oregon, where he is discovering new trails.

BERNIE SIEGEL

Love, Laughter, and the Nature of Life

AS A SURGEON who has worked with thousands of people with life-threatening illnesses, I have become aware of what is truly meaningful in our lives and what affects the process of healing. I also have had another experience that enlightened me. Several years ago I was selected to be an outside advisor to the Board of Directors of Heaven.

AT THE FIRST SESSION I ATTENDED, I noticed three plaques over God's desk. They read: *Don't feel personally, totally, eternally, irrevocably responsible for everything. That's my job; If you go around saying you have an awful life, I will show you what awful really is, and if you go around saying I have a wonderful life, I will show you what wonderful really is;* and *Everything you forget I remember, and everything you remember, I forget.*

I could see our Creator had a sense of humor, but I still couldn't see why God didn't make a perfect world free of problems so that we would all have an easier experience. I said to God one day, "I can't understand why you didn't make a perfect world."

"You are not God, so you can't understand. But consider this: a perfect world would be a magic trick and meaningless. Creation is work. It is as if you are all attending school and by learning about the nature of life can become complete like the animals. It is not an accident that after everything I created I said I saw that it was good, but when I created man I didn't say that. I want your actions to be meaningful. So when you share your love and create a sense of joy, it means something to your fellow man. If the world were like the Garden of Eden, it would all be expected and thus mean nothing. Yes, life has its dark side too, but every curse contains a blessing if you have the courage to seek it out."

"Another thing, tell your fellow man to stop wars and suicides because, as you can see, we have a housing problem here. Remember that when you give your report, the committee will know you are finished when you say, 'the beginning.'"

"Why say 'the beginning' and not 'the end?'"

"Because life is a series of beginnings, and when you finish your report, we will begin to use the information, just as graduations are not terminations but commencements, and the Bible ends in Revelation and not a conclusion."

AS I HAVE CONTINUED TO CARE FOR PEOPLE, I have seen that too often religion, parenting, and our education system lead to guilt, shame, and blame. When used or interpreted improperly, they become unhealthy parts of our upbringing. We truly need to awaken to the feelings and wisdom of our hearts. Love and laughter are the great healers, but too often we do not make time for them until we have little time left and accept our mortality.

We are all wounded. When people ask me, "How are you?" I answer, "Depressed. Out of my antidepressant and my doctor is away, so I can't renew my prescription." Eighty percent of people answer, "I know how you feel." Others offer me their antidepressants and more importantly share their pain with a stranger because they know I will understand. So remember: in love's service, only the wounded soldier can serve.

Despite our wounds, we can still laugh. The love and humor I talk about are childlike in nature. I learned that acting like a child helped me to see the world with joy and bring out the child in others. When I see a sign "Wet Floor," I wet the floor. When I receive a document with a sticker that says "Sign Here," I write "Here" on the paper. When I walk up to counters, I always say, "How may I help you?" to confuse the clerks. Today I drove to the drive-up window at our bank and gave the clerk a withdrawal slip for one dog biscuit. (They give out biscuits at the bank, and our dog enjoys them.) Sometimes at the bank window I ask, "Is my order ready?"

I could go on with my childlike behavior, but the greatest benefit to embarrassing your children when you eat out by ordering Italian food in a Chinese restaurant is that the children stop eating out with you, and you save a fortune. I will also find that when my children grow up and do something considered out of line, people say, "Do you know who his father is?" thus eliminating them from blame and making them happy to now have me for their father.

Through love and laughter, one maintains a sense of connection despite the difficulties of life. From that connection, a sense of self-esteem and self-worth are developed. By middle age, of those children who described their parents as loving, only twenty-five percent had suffered a major illness, while of those who said their parents were not loving, almost one-hundred percent had suffered a major illness.

People who own pets will smoke outdoors to protect their pets. They will kill themselves but not do anything to hurt their beloved pets. As Maimonides said centuries ago, "If we would treat ourselves as kindly as we treat our animals, we would suffer fewer illnesses." So adopt a pet and be as kind to yourself as you are to your pet.

Life is uncertain. Eat dessert first. Hope, love, and a sense of humor are vital to survival in the face of uncertainty. Volunteers and optimists live longer, healthier lives. People with spiritual support also are healthier, and I have had patients who had so-called incurable diseases disappear when they "left their troubles to God" or went home to "make the world beautiful" before they died. Do not try to not die. It doesn't work. In heaven, the bitterest people are the vegetarian, meditating joggers who wish they had slept late and tasted a lobster or steak.

Live your life as if you are going to die, and use your lifetime doing what feels good and makes you happy. In other words, live your "chocolate ice cream." The byproduct will be a longer, healthier life. Remember information does not change people, but inspiration does. Just as God breathed life into Adam's nostrils so are we to inspire ourselves and others. Whenever you have a decision to make, pay attention to how your body feels and what makes you happy. Then decide. Your heart is very wise, so do not think but feel.

LOVE IS A POWERFUL WEAPON. We can learn to kill with kindness and torment with tenderness. It is no accident that we are told to love, not like, our enemies. So remain in awe of the nature and wisdom of life and enhance it by bringing love and joy into your life. Our beliefs are our biology and alter the chemistry of the body. An actor in a comedy has low stress hormone levels and excellent immune function, but the same performer in a tragedy can be made sick because his immune function is altered by the role he or she is playing.

Therein lies the secret of life. If you never want to grow old, do something you love to do, so you lose track of time. If you don't know what time it is, you can't age, and it is the healthiest state you can be in. To help you to do this, I will tell you how I have accomplished it. On my wrist I wear a bracelet that reads "WWLD." What do you think that means? Think about it for a minute.

It relates to who my role model is: "What Would Lassie Do?" So whenever I have a decision, I ask myself, "What would Lassie do?" and I do it. You can get over depression by asking, "What would Lucy do?" and doing it. Find the correct role model and rehearse until you are Mother Teresa or whomever you model yourself after. Remember: how do you get to Carnegie Hall? Practice, practice, practice.

As the great Jewish philosopher Woody Allen said, "Life is full of miserableness, loneliness, unhappiness, and suffering, and it's all over much too quickly." Sit down and listen, and the word will come to you and enlighten you. Remember words used improperly can become wordswordswords, swords. We are all like blank canvases upon which we create a work of art. As Jeremiah observed while watching the potter, we are works in progress. There are no mistakes, and like the seasons there are reasons for the path we take and lessons to be learned. So keep reworking the clay until you get it right.

BERNIE SIEGEL, M.D., a retired general/pediatric surgeon and founder of Exceptional Cancer Patients, is now involved in humanizing medical care and medical education. He is the author of *Love, Medicine & Miracles; Peace, Love & Healing; How to Live between Office Visits;* and *Prescriptions for Living.* This fall *Help Me to Heal* and *365 Prescriptions for the Soul* (which he likes to think of as "soulutions" to help people every day) will be published. Bernie resides in Connecticut with his wife, Bobbie. His website is www.ecap-online.org.

PART III

Reconnecting

*Because our sense of who we are and our freedom
are interrelated,
whatever we do from our freedom
in accord with our thinking
becomes a permanent part of us.
Our inner self includes
everything that comes from our love
because our love is our life;
and whatever we do
because of our life's love, we do freely.*
—EMANUEL SWEDENBORG
  Divine Providence (paragraph 78)

MARGARET SZUMOWSKI

We Cannot Extinguish the Night

I love walking the backbone of the earth
and lying down with you.

You patiently show me again, Deneb,
Vega, and Altair, the Big Dipper ready

to scoop us up. Night whispers
to us to leap into the dipper and feel

the gust of his breath. We take the stars
for ourselves, Swan in Flight, Hercules,

Cassiopeia and Scorpion.
We take these stars and wear them

around our necks like David.
The well of the sky is holy.

We do not take anything
but a drink of bright water.

For once we will be content
with the light from our rough bodies,

fires that burn behind our closed eyelids,
desire we cannot extinguish.

After college, MARGARET SZUMOWSKI joined the Peace Corps. As a hostage in Uganda, she had the distinction of having her photo taken by Idi Amin—a sort of keepsake for him. Margaret received her MFA from the University of Massachusetts and is currently associate professor of English at Springfield Technical Community College. Her work has appeared in *Calyx, Willow Springs, American Poetry Review, Poetry East, The Agni Review,* and *River Styx,* as well as in a chapbook, *Ruby's Cafe,* and in her first book-length collection of poetry, *I Want This World.* She is the winner of the 2002 Peace Corps Writers Prize for Poetry.

PENNY SUSAN ROSE

The Manifold Manifestations

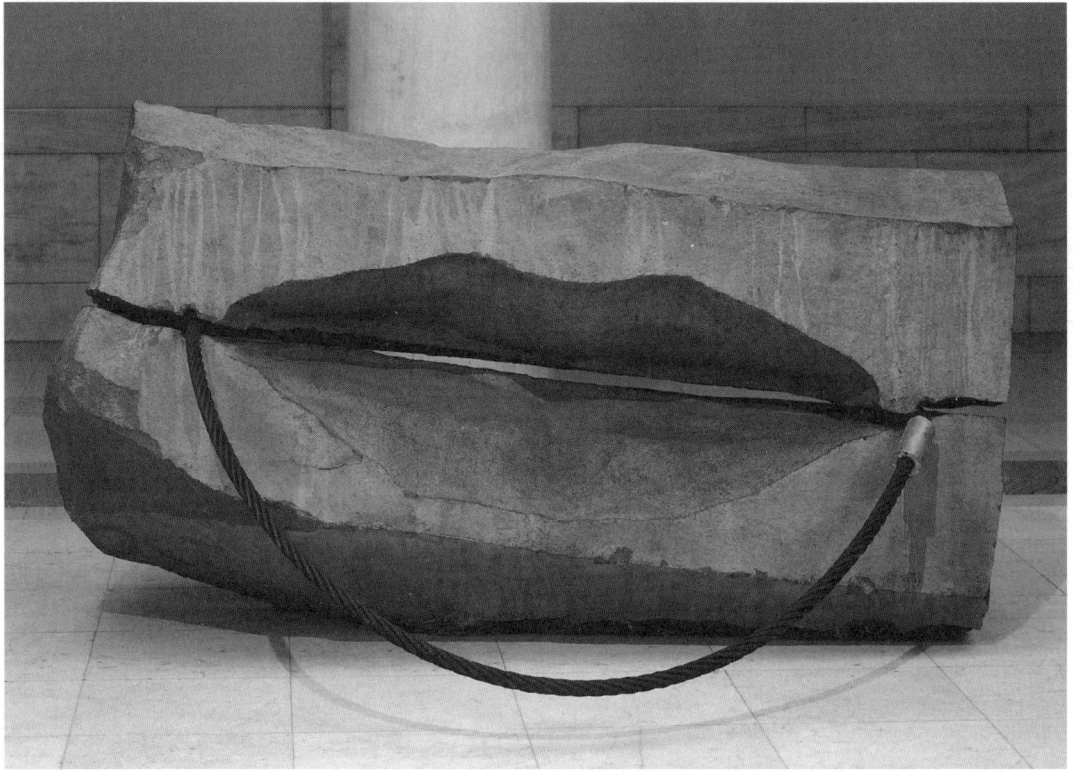

Luciano Fabro.
Demetra.
Stone and steel cable,
44.75×79.75×31 in.,
1987. San Francisco
Museum of Modern Art.
Gift of Robin Quist
in memory
of George Quist.

"YOU HAVE REACHED the offices of the Manifold Manifestations of the Universal Godhead."

The voice, youngish female, paused.

"Please listen closely to this menu of options as we frequently vary the prompts in an effort to better serve you."

Earlier that evening, Avery had surreptitiously memorized a catchy number, 1-800-GET-GOOD food, on the cover of a fabulous catalog.

There had been page after page of cheese—cheddar, mild and sharp, Gloucester, Muenster, Gouda, rounds and slices and blocks of cheese—and nuts—unshelled, salted in the shell, shelled, unsalted, roasted, mixed. Then there were sausages—weisswurst, duck and apple, spicy and mild Italian—then pâtés—and mousse truffeé, fois grâs and vegetable.

The fruit pages were gorgeous—moist golden pears and glistening red apples, green and yellow apples, then pineapples, red plums, black and purple plums, baskets of mixed fruit and canisters of dried fruit. Then the jellies and jams followed by page after page of desserts and fine chocolates. On the last few pages the fish—albacore tuna and whole salmon, poached or smoked, and then caviar—Sevruga or Beluga offered at incredibly reasonable prices when purchased with imported, crustless toast points and a bottle of Perrier Jouét champagne.

Avery's fiancée Amy had studied each page of the mail-order delicatessen, bemoaning their fate; it was too late to order and benefit from the great prices and the guaranteed-in-time-for-New-Year's-Eve delivery.

The voice on the phone recommenced, and behind it, faintly, Avery made out the sound of a harp, lightly stroked, melodious.

"If you know the extension of the Manifestation with which you seek to connect, you may enter that number at any time. For a directory of extensions, please press the star key. If you do not have a touch-tone phone and it pleases you to remain on the line, a Litanist will serve you."

Orders placed by phone or fax to The Good Food Company and paid by credit card no later than December 28 would be delivered anywhere in the continental United States in time for New Year's Eve. Avery was past the deadline but was willing to pay extra freight charges. Surely, a delivery could be arranged. Of course, he could pick something up at Say Cheese, but their prices were exorbitant compared to the Good Food deal, even including the freight. It seemed, however, that Avery had reached the wrong number.

The voice commenced again: "You have not pressed the star key, nor have you entered an extension. We remind you that a directory of extensions is available by pressing the star key or, if it pleases you, you may remain on the line and the first available Litanist will serve you."

Harp music increased in volume. Avery recognized the melody as Bach, a partita. Clearly, he had made a mistake, but he could not bring himself to hang up.

"We apologize for the extended delay, but due to the high volume of contacts, all Litanists are currently engaged. Your call is important to us and will be taken in the order received. If it pleases you, remain on the line or press the star key for a directory of extensions."

Avery pressed the star key.

There was a pause and then a new voice, male, low, and pleasant, said, "You have reached the directory of extensions for the Manifold Manifestations of the Universal Godhead. Please listen closely as we frequently vary the prompts in order to better serve you."

There was a pause.

"For the directory of the Myriad Manifestations of the male principle of the Universal Godhead, please press the star key now."

Avery pressed the star key.

There was a pause.

Then another voice, male, this time with a slight accent, Eastern European, Avery thought, or perhaps Indian: "You have reached the primary directory for the Myriad Manifestations of the male principle of the Universal Godhead.

> If you wish to connect with those manifestations known as Arjuna, Brahma, Bodhisattva, Atman, or Krishna, please press one.
> For Gautama, the Buddha, or Maitreya, please press two.
> For Ahura Mazda or Zarathustra, press three.
> For Moses the Prophet, Abraham, Isaac, Jacob, David, Jehovah, Adonai, or Yahweh, press four.
> For John the Baptist, Jesus the Christ, the Apostles, or the Messiah, please press five.
> For the Prophet Mohammed or Allah, press six.
> For Master Kung, Confucius, or Shang-ti, press seven.
> For Lao-tze or the Tao, press eight.
> For additional subdirectories, please press nine.
> For the primary directory of the Myriad Manifestations of the feminine principle of the Universal Godhead, please press the star key now."

A dizzying array of options. Clearly Avery had stumbled onto some New Age marketing organization, and the pitch would kick in soon, an offering of books about religion, myth, or meditation music on CD. Although Avery had missed the New Age wave, Amy loved to wander through the Bodhi Tree Bookstore, fingering crystals, examining runes and Tarot decks, sniffing at essential oils and incense. Avery decided to stick with it. Maybe it was a fortuitous mistake. Maybe they had something unusual, something Amy would really like. He would try the Good Food number again later.

"You have not entered an extension nor have you pressed the star key. You may return to the previous menu by pressing the pound sign now or, if it pleases you, remain on the line and the first available Litanist will serve you. Please enjoy this interlude of music."

The interlude was a choral presentation of "Jesu, Joy of Man's Desiring."

Avery pressed the star key.

A female, a strong-voiced soprano, spoke at once: "You have reached the primary directory of the Myriad Manifestations of the feminine principle of the Universal Godhead.

If you wish to connect with those Manifestations known as Yami, Gaia Meter, Shakti/Kali Ma, or Maya, please press one.
For Maha-Maya or Mara, press two.
For Mashya/Mashyoi, press three.
For Lilith, Eve, Sarah, Rebecca, Rachel, Leah, Tamar, or Miriam, press four.
For Mary Magdalene, Mary of Nazareth, please press five.
For Al-lat or Al-ilat, press six.
For Yin or Keang Yuen, press seven.
For the Dove, the Sow. . ."

Avery was overwhelmed. He pressed the pound key. There was a long pause and then: "This is the Litanist. Did you wish to return to the previous menu, or may I otherwise direct your call?"

The voice sounded older, female. There was a breathless, amused quality to it.

Avery was caught off guard.

"Oh!" he said, "you're not a recording!"

"There are no recordings in the office of the Manifold Manifestations. All contacts are personal."

"Those directories and listings were recordings, weren't they?"

"Oh, heavens no! The Litanies are live and constantly varied for your pleasure. We offer an infinite variety of potential contacts. Did you wish to review further directories? I have several more at my disposal. Something obscure or perhaps the Olympians?"

It was absurd, this whole thing, but intriguing too.

Avery said, "Chat with Zeus, you mean? You're saying if I want to speak to one of the . . . the . . ."

"Manifestations?"

" . . . the manifestations, you're suggesting that I would actually be speaking to that . . . to him . . . to it?"

"Yes! Absolutely!" She laughed. "No pun intended, Avery."

Avery sat up straight. He might have inquired further about the authenticity of the so-called manifestations but hearing his name put him on guard: "You know my name?"

"Oh, yes."

"That's disconcerting."

"I am sorry. I would have anticipated the opposite effect."

"What is it? I mean, Caller ID or something?"

"Yes, Caller ID," she responded with a throaty laugh. "In a manner of speaking."

Avery considered hanging up. He imagined an onslaught of late evening calls from rat-faced commission reps locked in airless cubicles with automatic dialers and phone lists that would now include his unlisted number and his name. Charges to the tune of five dollars and ninety-five cents a minute might now be mounting on his telephone bill.

"Avery?"

"I'm here," he said.

"Is there a Manifestation with which you would particularly like to connect?"

"How much is this costing me?"

"Our service is entirely free of charge."

"No kidding?"

"No kidding."

"To tell you the truth . . ." he started to say.

"We always appreciate that," she interjected with amusement.

"I'm a little unclear as to what exactly your service entails. I was calling to order caviar and champagne for New Year's Eve."

"Perhaps Dionysus then?"

Avery caught the murmur of voices laughing quietly.

He said, "I mean to say that I thought I was calling somewhere else. This whole thing is really completely unintentional."

"We don't subscribe to the notion of the unintentional here, Avery."

"Ooookay. Let me ask you this then. What exactly are you selling?"

"Selling?" She sounded genuinely puzzled. "Oh! You mean, like the caviar?" Her voice went lower then, less amused but still kindly, "Not a thing, Avery."

"Then, I'd like to know, what is the point of all this?"

"*That*," she replied earnestly, "is of course one of the most frequently asked questions, but it is best addressed to one of the Manifold Manifestations."

Avery could not penetrate the ploy. He had been on the phone for some time. She had reeled him in, and it was mildly disturbing to him that he had allowed it, but he liked this woman, her throaty amused voice.

"Avery?"

"I'm here."

"Is there a Manifestation with whom I can connect you now? Your question is a good one."

"Which question?" Avery could not recall that he had asked a question.

"About the point of, as you put it, all this."

"Can't *you* tell me?"

"Oh!" She sounded pleasantly surprised. "It is not my assigned function. I am merely a Litanist."

"Will you try?"

"Can you excuse me for a moment?"

"Sure."

There was a murmur of voices, muffled, as if she had put her hand over the mouthpiece. He had obviously thrown them—he was thinking in terms of a corporate "them"—a curve.

"Avery?"

"Yes."

"I've obtained special permission to address your question. I want first to thank you for directing it to me. It is a very great honor." She sounded inordinately pleased.

"You're welcome," he said, thinking: "Here it comes."

He noticed, then, a mild tingling at the tip of his spine. He reached back reflexively and scratched the spot.

"The point, Avery, is to awaken. The point is, put very simply, to be."

That was all she said. Meanwhile, the tingling sensation began to spread. It moved genially up Avery's spine, as if a warm hand were touching him and each vertebra, as the hand moved past, held the impress of it, a mild warmth lingering.

"To be what?"

"Just simply to be."

"I don't follow."

The tingling warmth spread, slowly, like lava, articulating Avery's skeleton and then his musculature. He felt it everywhere, superficially as warmth on his skin, and then deeply, as radiant heat in his bones. It spread to his internal organs. It was as if they suddenly lit up in his mind, each separate but connected, and visibly functioning. He felt transparent, like the clear plastic model of the human body he had once received for his birthday when he was a boy. His veins were royal blue and red, coming and going from his rhythmically heaving, deep magenta heart muscle. His liver was plump, moist and brownish-purple. His brain was pinkish-gray, and electrical bursts crackled over its surface when she spoke again.

"It is perhaps too simple to comprehend, caught as you are in your present idea."

Avery could barely respond. He sensed the whole of his body engaged in the apprehension of her words and the highly complex preparations for the subsequent regurgitation of his response.

"My present idea?"

"Perhaps if you were willing to conceive of the notion that your life is limited by your preconceptions you would begin to understand."

"Meaning that I have certain belief systems?"

As Avery uttered that sentence, he sensed, as never before, the formation of words in his head. In a quite specific area of his pinkish-gray brain, electrical impulses palpably erupted, synapses fired, nerve endings pulsed motivating muscles, breath moved, and his throat vibrated as his tongue wagged.

"Yes!" She spoke excitedly. "Exactly! You see that there are constructs, arbitrary, cultural, learned or inherited. Your worldview is habitual, a prefabrication that limits perception. Do you understand?"

A strange progression of thought commenced for Avery. He *had* formulated a worldview, though he did not often think of it. It was simplistic, a horizontal progression, rather bleak as he reviewed it now in this state of heightened sensitivity. A man was born. He lived. If he was inherently good, he did mostly good things, or at least nothing much that was bad, in his lifetime. If he was fortunate, a preponderance of good things and not too many awful things happened to him. Then, he died. Finito.

Avery realized that other lines of thought, caviar and champagne, marketing ploys and sales traps, had not completely fallen away, but his awareness of the physical, sensational progression of his thought subsumed them. He felt himself thinking! It was happening in his body, this thinking. It was an extraordinary, nearly miraculous, and highly peculiar self-intimacy, never before experienced, transforming processes of thought and emotion experienced in the crucible of his body.

"I sense," she said, "that you begin to understand." Her voice was all breath, with an edge of excitement. "You see that awareness of being commences as sensation? This is being, Avery. This is how it feels in your body."

A wave of emotion broke over him, wild exhilaration, unexpected and conflicted; it was uncontainable. It filled Avery up. It was joy, immense, but tremendously fragile, and so, simultaneously, unimaginably poignant.

"You see that you are, yourself, the key. The sensation of your body is your link to this moment and to each succeeding moment, and so to all of us here, to the Manifold Manifestations of the Universal Godhead. You do see, don't you?"

Avery did see. He was afraid to speak for fear of losing the remarkable sensation.

"It is tenuous, we know. So-called thought and feeling will interfere. They heave to the future, cleave to the past, to your constructs and the habitual, but sensation is always available. The link that you have made is available because your physical body is always, absolutely, in the moment. Do you see Avery?"

Her voice had receded slightly.

The fineness of his perception was now almost painful to him, and Avery did see. He saw thoughts arising in his brain, bubbles above the head of a cartoon character. Each thought sought to claim him, draw him into definition, into an idea, a construct. He was sensing, second to second now, the danger; how easily he could be drawn away from this immensity, seduced from clarity and the sensation of being into some limited view, some appetite, some inanity.

"I've never experienced this," said Avery, sensing his hand wrapped around the handset, sensing his ear warm against the plastic. "It's like I'm inside and outside myself all at once."

"But you have experienced it, you know," she said in gentle reprimand. "When you were an infant, you experienced this connection all the time. It was natural to you. That is why we know you by name, Avery. The Christ often mentions 'the little children' when people speak with him. He is reminding them of the simplicity of the child that they still carry within, the ability of the child to enter into a moment entirely, to treat it as play."

"This is play?" said Avery, doubt in his voice.

"It *is* play," she said, "although maintaining it may later seem to be work. There is prayer, of course, of many kinds. Many people find that helpful. There is meditation. There are various kinds of work with the breath and certain types of movement. It is all in aid of the same thing."

"In aid of being?"

"Yes, Avery."

"To what end?"

"Unification."

"Of?"

"Of yourself and, therefore, of the Manifold Manifestations of the Universal Godhead. In those terms, the endeavor to be, to unify, is in the service of your Creator. Understanding *that* requires time and study. It is a much larger understanding than what we have attempted here, Avery."

Her voice was definitely lower, as if she had moved a distance away.

Unavoidably, thoughts of Amy ascended in Avery's head and then the Good Food catalog and the number he had intended to dial. It was a cascade of the mundane. Avery sensed, at once, a decline of sensation, a decline in his awareness of his body. He struggled to maintain the connection. It did not feel like play.

She spoke, and the volume of her voice was lower still. "The larger intention is symbolized in your physical world in thousands of wonderful ways. The word 'love' is such a symbol, often signified by representations of the pierced heart muscle or the cruciform, sometimes by animal representations, and, of course, there is the white rose."

Avery felt as if he were drowning. He could barely hear her now for a thrumming in his head.

"We sense your struggle Avery. Remember it. Know that, even without understanding, it is enough for now to simply strive for sensation."

"I'm losing it!" he cried out.

"It cannot be lost, only misplaced. Thank you for giving me this opportunity to be of service to you, Avery. Thank you."

Her voice had faded out as if someone had been gradually turning down the volume on a stereo. The telephone line went dead.

"Wait!"

Quite suddenly and loudly, Avery heard the dial tone. He set the phone down in its cradle.

His body was inert, a lump, except for a slight buzz on the surface, as if he had goose pimples all over. He felt bereft. What had happened to him? Avery glanced at his watch and knit his brow.

The conversation had seemed long, a half or at least a quarter of an hour. He had sat down and dialed the number at roughly nine o'clock but now, the second hand of his watch was just progressing away from the hour.

Had it been a dream? Had he nodded off at his desk and made up the whole extraordinary episode?

No. He had definitely dialed the phone. He would have been ordering later than the deadline, but it had seemed worth the effort. Amy had been so excited by the pictures in the catalog. He would have happily paid extra for priority overnight delivery just to see the expression of pleasure and surprise on her face.

"Too bad we're too late," she had said, closing the catalog, and from that point on Avery had been plotting.

His thoughts returned, seamlessly, to these ordinary paths. They felt comfortable, worn as old slippers warped to the shape of his feet. His recollection of the exhilaration, the sensations of joy and of danger from seconds before were blunted. There was just enough left of the extraordinary awareness so that he could faintly recall the difference.

He sat at his desk looking at the telephone. All he had to do was punch the redial button, and he would be reconnected.

Suddenly the phone rang!

Avery grabbed the handset before the first ring had ended.

"Sweetheart?"

"Amy!"

"Have you been running? You sound out of breath. Listen, darling..."

She rushed on to tell him that she had done a monumental shopping for their New Year's Eve feast. She would roast Cornish game hens, she said, stuffed with wild rice. She had found beautiful white asparagus. She had bought their favorite Chardonnay and was making a pear and brandy tart.

The impulse to tell her about the strange call evaporated as she prattled on. How could Avery explain what had happened? Already, the substance and the shape of it, the voices, the music, even the extraordinary character of his sensation had receded exactly as dreams do on waking. No time had passed. He had verified that by his watch. It had been amazingly vivid, but he had no words to explain it, and it was almost gone now, almost entirely gone.

"Sorry you have to work tomorrow," said Amy. "We'll make up for it in the evening. You'll see."

"See you by seven," he said.

"Love you," said Amy.

"You too," and he punched the hook to disconnect.

Suddenly, aggressively, Avery punched the redial button. He heard beep-tones and then the ring. He held his breath.

"Thank you for calling Good Food. All of our representatives are busy with other customers, but your call is very important to us and will be taken in the order received. Please hold for the next available sales associate."

Avery hung up as a mechanized rendition of "Auld Lang Syne" began to play in his ear.

The next day was December 31st. Avery worked at the office, completing a report for his boss. He felt out of sorts, peculiar. He screwed up the data in his spreadsheet and had to rebuild a whole section of it. He was strangely forgetful and short-tempered. He had not slept well, and his general uneasiness carried through to the evening when he found himself at Amy's door empty-handed. He had completely forgotten to buy champagne, caviar, flowers, candy, anything. He felt like a total idiot, but it was too late to remedy the situation.

When Amy opened the door, however, she was visibly excited. She grabbed Avery's hand. She kissed him, pulling him at once into the dining room.

Soft music played in the background. Three tall silvery candles were burning in elegant crystal holders, and sparks of light reflected from the white china and the polished silver. Amy danced at the end of the dining table that she had set, so beautifully, for their dinner. There was a package sitting on the edge of the table.

"Fed-Ex delivered it," she said. "It's addressed to you. You know what it is, don't you? May I open it?"

Amy wore a simple beige silk dress. Her cheeks were flushed, and her eyes were bright with excitement, her brown hair fell over her shoulders. The scent of delectable food was in the air—hens browning, aromatic rice, and hot bread.

Amy is so lovely, Avery thought, and there was a subtle shift in his mood. He was suffused with a sense of well-being, but it made him, strangely, pause inside. How quickly he moved from mood to mood, state to state. I am an idiot. I am delighted. He wondered if there was anything of substance in him, anything immutable.

The simple brown-wrapped package bore a plain white label, addressed by hand in florid script, to Avery in care of Amy. There was no return address.

Amy's hands were fluttering above it, birds seeking to light.

"I've no idea what it is," said Avery. He moved closer to Amy put his arm around her waist and breathed in the scent of her. "Open it!"

Amy tore away the wrappings, opened the carton.

White paper frothed out like champagne bubbles from a fluted glass.

Avery's heart began to pound in his chest. Tingling warmth moved up his spine.

"Oh Avery," breathed Amy, "how sweet! You managed it after all."

Avery sensed the soles of his feet and each toe inside his shoes, his breath moving in and out, his heart going bu-bump, bu-bump in his chest. He leaned over to see what nestled in the froth of paper.

There was a tin of Beluga caviar, a box of imported, crustless toast points, a bottle of Perrier Jouét, and in a cunning silver holder, a single, quite perfect, highly scented, white rose.

PENNY SUSAN ROSE has been writing short stories, essays, and poetry for years. Her stories have appeared in *Lumina* and in *Westview* and one is forthcoming in *The Distillery*. She has two completed novels in hiding and a third in the works.

VINCENT DECAROLIS

William My Friend

Something I never expected
is how welcome I feel
at the plot where my parents are buried
and up the lane a little too
where Bill, who used to teach math
in the room next to mine, also lies
beneath a simple stone.

He liked my poems.
I liked the way he figured in his head,
as if the numbers were floating
in the air above his brow.

Myself, I've always been slow when it
comes to calculations, feeling instead
how in November the leaves are
giving up and in April how dark roots
stir because the ground is whispering.

Here we are then,
Bill, who could solve for X
like a hound on a scent,
and I, who can solve for nothing,
talking through some kind of
one-way glass
with my mother and father
behind him eager for news.

VINCENT DECAROLIS devotes most of his time to writing poetry and fiction. His scholarly interests include the collected works of C.G. Jung, New Testament studies, and James Joyce. In winter he likes to snowshoe with his wife and, when not writing, enjoys painting (mostly in acrylics and mixed media). His short story "Claims" appeared in the Chrysalis Reader *Seeing Through Symbols*.

BARBARA WALKER

The Decision

THE BUS RUMBLED AWAY leaving a cloud of exhaust in its wake. The women sitting on the bench put her hand over her mouth so she wouldn't inhale the fumes. As the quiet returned, she lowered her head and slumped, her posture one of misery and defeat.

Marie had watched three buses come and go. As people came and waited for the next bus, they glanced at her with curious expressions. None of them approached her, however, and she had the bench to herself.

From time to time, she shook her head and wondered why she couldn't make up her mind to either get on the bus or take herself on up that hill behind her. She noticed that no passengers ever got off the incoming buses. Perhaps it was a sign that no one really wanted to go up there.

Alone again, she turned and looked up the hill. About a quarter mile from where she sat, stood the administrative building of the convent. A paved, winding driveway led from the road up to the convent, and the occasional delivery truck weaved its way up and down as she sat at her post.

Marie knew she needed to get on with something—her life, the bus ride, anything. All she managed to do, though, was sit there. She was seized with indecision. Should she start walking toward the small religious community or climb on the next bus?

She was dressed in a shabby coat, which only partially covered well-worn but laundered slacks and tennis shoes. Her hard-sided suitcase was on the ground in front of her. Despite the blustery day, her head was bare, revealing short, graying black hair.

"I can't do it, Lord," she prayed. "I just can't go there. Please help me."

She knew there was an answer somewhere to her lack of purpose and resolve. She felt sure that those who lived up on that hill would

L.S. Lowry.
The Empty House.
Oil on plywood, 1934.
Stoke-on-Trent, City Museum and Art Gallery.

try to help her through it. Then again, maybe they couldn't. She had to work this through herself.

Up until a few weeks ago, she had been so sure of her faith and the direction this faith would take her. Those few confidants who felt comfortable speaking bluntly would often say, "I wish I could be more like you, Marie, so determined and self-assured." She could never figure out what this meant. She was simply who she was. What was the big deal? Until lately, that is. She couldn't pinpoint when this self-doubt had started or even what was causing it.

Maybe the world has just caught up with me, she thought. Soon, she ceased to debate with herself and just let her mind drift with the leaves and dust kicked up by the small whirlwinds that blew past her.

After a while, another bus approached. A person got off this time, a young girl about twenty or so. Marie watched as the driver got out, pulled a good-sized duffel bag from the storage area, and handed it to the new arrival. The girl picked up her suitcase and looked up the hill.

The bus pulled back into the road and began its slow departure. The girl turned and made as if to stop the bus, then changed her mind and stood by the curb. After a while, she looked over to the bench and noticed Marie sitting there.

She came over and asked, "Do you mind if I sit here?" Marie did not reply, just smiled and moved over to make some room. The girl sat at the very end of the bench, with her duffel bag on the ground beside her. As people unconsciously mimic the pose of others, the girl also sat with shoulders hunched and head hanging. They were like bench bookends, dual portraits of indecision and misery.

After a while, Marie's curiosity got the best of her. "Are you here to enter the convent?"

The response was a nod of the head. Another minute passed, and the girl asked, "Why didn't you get on the bus?"

Marie shrugged. This was a hard one to answer. "It looks like we're in the same boat," offered Marie. "Neither of us can make up our minds either to go up the hill or get on the next bus."

The girl looked at her. "With all due respect, ma'am, you seem a little old to be entering convent life." She reddened as she said this, knowing it was borderline rude, but it was too late to take it back.

Marie didn't take offense. She was feeling every one of her years lately and still remembered how she had looked at older people when she was the same age as this youngster.

"I'm supposed to begin my aspirancy today," the girl explained. She went on to clarify to Marie that becoming an aspirant is the very first step in entering religious life. "After a period of time, if things work out, the next step is to become a postulant," she explained as she gazed up the hill.

"Where's your family?" asked Marie. "This is a big step to go through by yourself." She knew now that she was the one being borderline rude, but she felt an urgency to know what was happening with this girl. She tried to soften her question by introducing herself. "My name's Marie, by the way. I seem to not be in a hurry to go anywhere myself today, so we can talk if you want while we both wait for inspiration."

"Oh, they wanted to come all the way, but I wouldn't let them. I wanted to do this last part of the trip by myself. Mom was real upset and kept saying, 'Please Anne, let us take you right up to the door.' But somehow I just wanted to be alone, you know, right before."

"Before?" thought Marie. She was getting the impression that Anne was acting like someone entering jail instead of a convent.

Anne, who seemed thankful to have someone to talk to, explained that, now that she was here, on the brink, she was getting cold feet. She was suddenly afraid to make the trek up that hill, to face the challenges of convent life.

"Well, that makes two of us," murmured Marie more to herself than to Anne.

"What if I fail?" asked Anne, becoming more upset by the minute. "What if I try and try and just can't do it?" Tears dropped onto her cheeks as she looked over at Marie.

Marie was alarmed now and slid over to be a little closer to her seat-mate. She waited a short while, then handed over her last clean tissue.

"Anne, tell me, first of all, what made you decide to join the convent. Why did you want to be a part of it?"

Anne looked up at Marie and thought about her answer before responding. "It started more as a feeling when I was in high school. I felt a connection. I guess you could say, that was more than something you experience when you're in church or just praying. I mean, I didn't hear voices or anything like that, but I've always felt more complete when I was talking with God. I thought I wanted to spend my life serving God in the best way I could. But now, I'm not sure."

"So? What's changed to make you feel now that this may not be for you?" asked Marie. She knew she was addressing her own angst but couldn't stop herself.

Anne stood up and began pacing in front of their bench. "School came easy to me. I had the best grades, and I made the dean's list throughout college, but this, well, I just don't know. There's so much that'll be new and different. What if I can't do it? I mean, what if I don't measure up after all?"

Marie, having the benefit of years on her side, was pretty good at judging people. She knew that this young woman was intelligent and determined, despite her words.

"But here you are," she said.

"Yes, here I am," said Anne. "I did make the trip, but now I'm not exactly sure why."

"Perhaps because your faith kept you going. Without actually thinking about it, your faith was larger than your fears. It helped you get on that bus, and it helped you get off to make your walk up that hill." Marie felt her own burden begin to lift.

"Maybe," said Anne after a little while. She sat back down and looked at Marie. "Is this faith something that comes to a person as they get older? How do you know if you have enough faith or if you just don't measure up?"

"There you go again with the measuring up," Marie said. "Ask yourself, who is it you want to measure up to? The others up there in the convent? Your family? When you think about it, it's really between you and God."

Marie leaned back now, and for the first time in a long time, felt some of the old peacefulness.

"I get it," replied Anne, becoming excited. "All that God wants from me is to stay the course. He won't give me more than I can handle." She looked over at Marie with a smile that lit up her face.

"Yes, everyday can be a new test of just how far you can go with God as your partner."

"But we must learn to let go and let God take care of our spiritual progress," finished Marie.

Now it was clear to both of them that Marie's words were for herself as well as for her young friend. Marie reached over to hug Anne.

Just then, another bus came into view. Both women looked at it, then at each other. Without a word, they stood, picked up their luggage, and climbed the hill. When they got to the first building, Anne started up the steps.

When Marie didn't follow, she turned and looked.

"Have you changed your mind?" she asked with a note of fear creeping back in.

"No. I want to walk a bit more before I go in, that's all," replied the older woman. "You go on. I'm sure we'll see each other in a while."

A few hours later, as part of her entrance into the convent, Anne was ushered into the office of the Mother Superior. She wasn't looking forward to having to talk with this authority figure and was feeling intimidated as she approached the large desk for the first time.

It was the crown on a day she would never forget, and she understood what the older woman had realized down at the bus stop; God will always help us find a way home.

"Welcome, Anne," said Marie. "Most of the people here refer to me as Mother. . . ."

A full-time writer following many years of work in social services, BARBARA WALKER focuses on stories, articles, and essays dealing with the human condition. Utilizing the premise of writing what you know, her published work has addressed such issues as the challenges of caregiving and the trials and tribulations of the menopause experience.

BLAYNEY COLMORE

Reunion

Last weekend I came face to face with an
old demon.
Not the members of my high school class, all but
one of whom I hadn't seen for 47 years,
but the school itself, haunted site of my
adolescent collapse.

When I was 13, living in
the Philippines,
I was sent to my father's
old school in Connecticut.
His father had been friends with the monk who founded
the school,
my uncle was a faculty member,
my father had been head prefect and his brothers all
graduated.

I flunked out.

Shame and embarrassment replaced my family as my closest
companions.

So when email put me back in touch with
my classmates
I screwed up my courage, begged
Lacey to go with me, and went to my class'
45th reunion.

Good thing, it turns out, that I waited
this long.
This group of super-credentialed men,

U.N. weapons inspector, CIA leader, Olympic gold medalist, president of a Korean University, judge in the D.C. court, scions of Wall Street, head of a school in Greece, corporate

lawyers, a poet
were also now my
age
stepping gingerly onto the
western slope
more focused on what to make of it all now than on how we
got there.

Before dinner Saturday night, while the
younger classes
postured about the bar
networking
our class gathered on a terrace and spoke in measured
muted old men's voices
about our concern for our world and our nation, which many
of them
have borne significant responsibility for
shaping.

I went with my head
held low
expecting to slither in and quickly
out
of a scene I still sometimes dream about.

Instead I connected
with friends
old good friends
compassionate, vulnerable, open
old men
prepared at last to face our fear
of failure
and while we still have
breath explore the wounds we have received and
caused.

BLAYNEY COLMORE was an Episcopal parish priest for thirty years. His vision of a creation in which our species is subject to serendipity created consternation and delight among parishioners and continues to feed his curiosity about the purpose of ego in the ongoing evolution of the cosmos. Blayney sends, to those interested, periodic e-mails, "Notes from Zone 10" (California) and "Notes from Zone 4" (Vermont). *In The Zone: Notes on Wondering Coast to Coast* (2002) is available from Xlibris and major outlets. He can be reached at blayneyc@earthlink.net.

LANI WRIGHT

Druid Arch

WHEN I REACHED THE TURNOFF TO DRUID ARCH in Canyonlands National Park, I had already walked nine miles. It would be four "extra" miles roundtrip. Should I? Did I have the energy? I lingered a moment to pull out my water bottle and drink. The Utah sun was now a shade less brilliant than it had been at midday. The shadows longer, the light on the hoodoos—sandstone outcrops carved by nature into fantastic shapes—more golden.

I considered the three things I knew about Druid Arch. I liked the name. The Utah radical Mormon writer, Terry Tempest Williams, had gone there and written memorably about the trip in *Desert Quartet*. And my friend Gene, who has been everywhere, had never made it up to the Arch and hungered to do so.

I turned up the wash and began to climb. I was in the autopilot phase of walking. It was not that I didn't feel pain. My right hip creaked with every step. And the small toe on my left foot, which had blistered the week before, was, from the feel of it, reblistering under the old callus. When I let my attention roam the nooks and crannies of my body, there was pain. Mostly, though, I had stopped thinking. My mind was as uncluttered as a monk's cell. I was all light and bird song. Breath. Heart beat.

I stepped through the sand, scrambling up and over the occasional boulder, jumping from rock to rock, sidling past sprawling cacti. The monumental mushrooms of red rock topped with white caps had ceased to amaze me. All day I had been threading my way through these eroded spires that earlier gave rise to much anthropomorphic musings. Ah! That one. It looks like a king on a throne. And this one is a dead ringer for ET.

I stopped for more water. The desert seemed to suck it straight from my cells. The Colorado Plateau is so dry—only a few inches of rain fall per year, and sometimes all in one summer thunderstorm.

Frederic Edwin Church. *Natural Bridge, Virginia.* Oil on canvas, 38×33 in. (framed), 1852. University of Virginia Art Museum. Gift of Thomas Fortune Ryan.

Yet the fantastic forms looming around me, wrought through erosion, were mostly fabricated during rare, brief squalls and by the ever-present wind.

The route began to steepen. I climbed up a dry waterfall on all fours, clambering across the rock like an animal and then left the wash altogether. The trail seemed to go only up now—over rock, gravel, sand, and scree. I hopped back and forth through the labyrinth of footpaths seeking the easiest route. There was no arch in sight, but I am of the faithful—this day at least—and I followed the cairns as if they were religious monuments. The trail crossed a ledge, skirted a huge boulder, and there it was. Perfectly named. Fashioned from one massive block, the image from Stonehenge blown up to epic proportions. Two great stone monoliths supporting a huge stone lintel.

No one was there to watch as I climbed to sit beneath it and tempt fate under a zillion tons of sandstone—not such sturdy stuff as rock goes. I stared into space and sky, and clouds. But the view was too big. Waves of vertigo made me tremble. I shut my eyes. All was silence except the wind that rocked me gently from side to side.

I recalled a moment from my childhood when I had gone into my mother's bedroom to find her sitting in my grandmother's rocker and had climbed onto her lap. I was much too big to fit there anymore, but she let me come. I draped myself across her breast, and she put her arms around my waist to hold me in place. My face nuzzled her neck with its soft silky talcum smell. We rocked.

Just a glimmer of memory. A moment when I trusted completely. Was it possible at forty-seven to get back to this kind of faith?

I opened my eyes for another peek at the vast, turning universe—so steady in its motion. Then I looked up to the tons of stone towering above me—so oblivious to my mortality.

If one can still experience awe, maybe faith is recoverable, too, though perhaps not instantaneously. Faith implies a kind of neverending work, someplace deep, like the bottom of a well, where the blue sky is a faraway circle of color. Faith is the hard and endless work of constant reorientation from choices made in fear to choices made from love. But here, now, sheltered beneath the ancient weight of precariously balanced stone, anything seemed possible.

I had miles to go to reach my designated campsite where I'd pitch my tent and wait for the moon to rise. My warm body had chilled in the wind. I climbed down and shouldered my pack. A few minutes on the trail, and the arch disappeared from view. I hopped from rock to rock, listened to the dried yucca rattling like a medicine gourd in the wind. I left the arch to be discovered by whoever came next—any wayfarer whose mind was not preoccupied by too long, too tired, too late. Anyone whose heart was open to why not.

LANI WRIGHT has spent the last thirty-four years exploring and photographing the far-flung spaces of our planet. To date, she has visited sixty-three countries and all seven continents. In the past ten years, she has been drawn back to the Canyonlands region of the American southwest four times. In between travels, she directs a short-term teacher-training course for an international school in Brattleboro, Vermont, where she lives with her dog, Rosie.

WENDY L. BROWN

Coyote Fool Moon

SANDALED FEET ON ASPHALT, I am holding hands in a circle with seven people. I am struck by the incongruity of beginning a weekend of healing with this blessing in a parking lot. But I know it is the first strand in the weaving of the circle, a circle encompassing us within sacred time and space. I close my eyes and feel the mild morning sun on my face, take a few deep breaths, and promise myself to park all expectations.

This overnight workshop is created by Earthwalks for Health, a nonprofit organization to learn traditional ways of healing and being on the land. Entitled "Coyote Fool Moon," it sounds like a time of playfulness and surprises. The coyote in Native American tradition is the Trickster—mischievous, cunning, foolish but wise in getting us to laugh at our own self-importance. Little do I know what coyote has in store for me.

Arriving at Buck's house two hours later, I find that the outside is hot but the inside cool. Rowena and a figure draped in black lace stand in the doorway. "Hello," I say cheerfully. The tall, hidden figure bows, and Rowena blesses me with a prayer stick.

We begin with a game of "Photographer and Camera" by pairing up with someone we don't know. When my partner suggests I be the camera first, I immediately have to give up my desire to be in control. "Me first?" I gulp, but I surrender and close my eyes.

I can't reach out my hands and find my own boundaries but have to trust my guide to steer me. Hesitant at first, the pressure of her arm around my waist and the low voice giving me explicit instructions enable me to move with confidence. After positioning my body and head precisely, she says, "Open," and I open my eyes to a startling image. A snapshot indeed! Each is an unexpected treat, from the

Opposite:
Francisco Zuniga.
Mujer de Pie Con Manos en la Cara.
Bronze,
81⅛×21⅝×17⅞ in.,
1976. University of Arizona Museum of Art, Tucson. Museum purchase with funds provided by the Edward J. Gallagher, Jr. Memorial Fund.

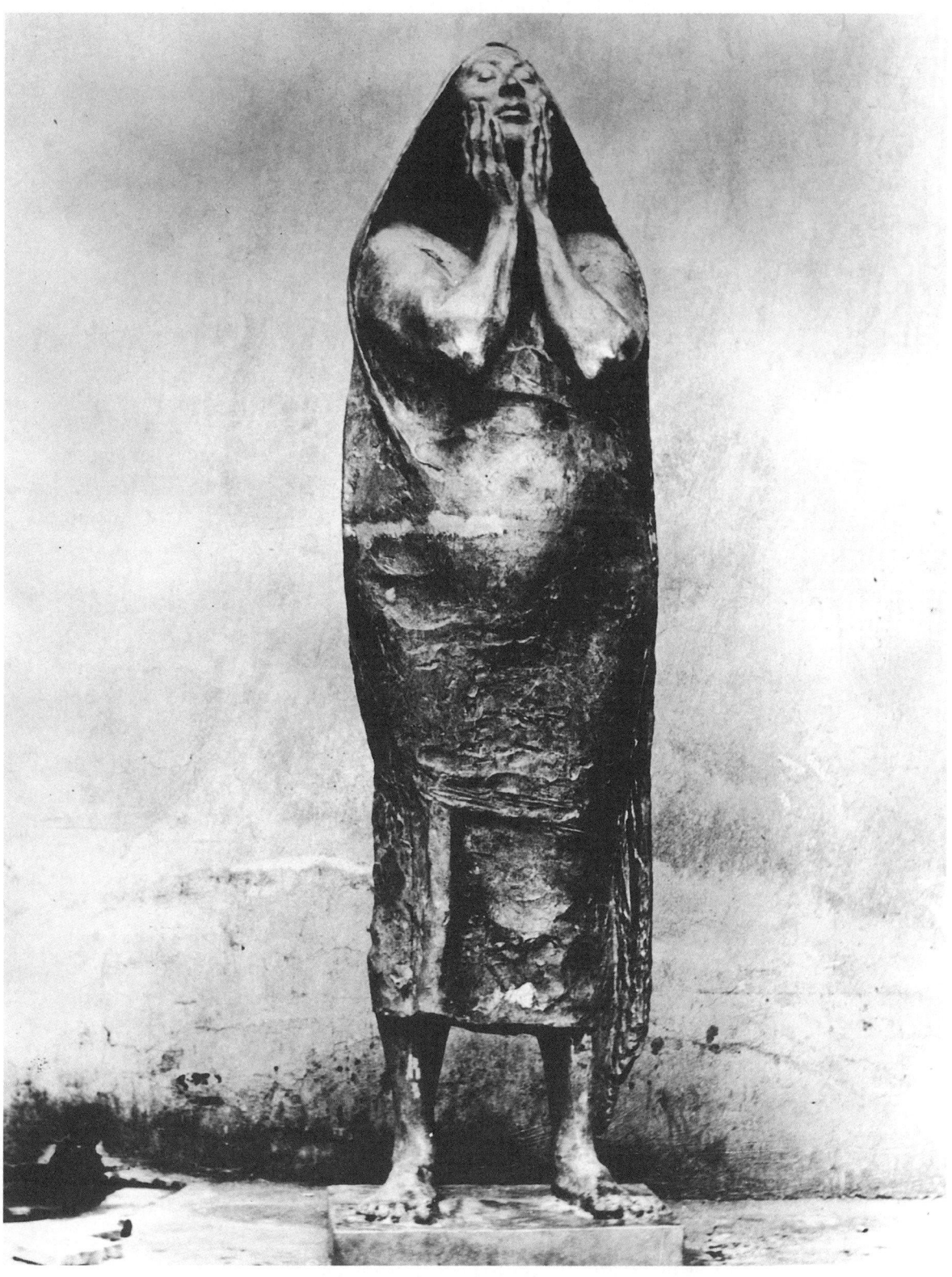

drum hanging in a corner to the panoramic view of the landscape outside. At one point, my eyes open to another couple, one of whom, a friend, is the "camera." Her eyes are still shut as she is led about, and I laugh heartily.

We reverse roles, and I realize how difficult it is to be the guide, to anticipate the rock under her foot before my "camera" steps on it, to get her to "snap" the shot I see so clearly. Steering her back to the house, her arm bumps against the door frame, and I know that she has been more exact and careful with me than I with her, how safe I had been.

Seated within a circle, I am intrigued by what people have to say. We begin with an introduction of the persons who were our "camera." They state their intention for the weekend and choose a colored candle to light. We laugh, muse, find consonance and communion in our desires for relaxation, rest, peace, letting go, change. Our guides, Rowena and Buck, have hearty laughs. Rowena is soft, maternal, humble, deep. Buck sits solidly as a rock with an inner focused peacefulness but also a sense of mischief and playfulness.

I mention the transition I am passing through without revealing those details held quietly in my heart, from nanny to writer, from youth to menopause, the attempt to manifest my dreams. I am here with my partner Michael who suffers from acute depression, and I hope the weekend will alleviate some of the suffering and rejuvenate me. I pick a white candle for divine guidance and peace. Later, when it is his turn to light a candle, Michael unknowingly relights the same one that the wind had blown out.

After lunch, the work begins. Advised to put on shorts, hats, and sunscreen, we women gather by the river. In groups of three, we are handed small vials of paint and are instructed to paint on ourselves the things we want to release into the river. My group is silent as we form a circle. I am surprised by how many things I want to let go of and paint both my arms and legs.

The men arrive a little later. One of the participants uses a walker and is assisted through the willows. While the women are already telling each other the meaning of their images, the men are painting on themselves and each other. "A different tribe," I joke and am suddenly transported back to an ancient ritual of decorating the skin in symbols, ceremonies of puberty rites, marriage, war-making, healing, creating tribal solidarity. Maybe they used dyes from berries and ashes from the fire, engraving the symbols with a sharp pointed stick, creating permanent tattoos, or maybe only for the occasion to be washed away in water and blood. As we tell each other the meaning of our symbols, I am again struck by the consonance. I could have painted any of the other's on my own body.

After the ritual of washing off the paint, we splash and play in the river. I am content to sit on a rock like a lizard in the sun with my feet in the cool, rushing water, watching peacefully, preparing myself for the next ceremony—a sweat lodge, an ancient ritual for cleansing and purging.

I have never participated in an authentic sweat and am torn between trepidation and anticipation. What if I feel suffocated, claustrophobic, sick from the heat? I don't easily feel comfortable with strangers, especially naked male strangers. The rules are not rigid. We can step out by saying, "I am called elsewhere"; we can sit close to the door, and clothing or nakedness is optional. The sweat lodge is styled "Apache Two Souls," meaning the male and female, light and shadow, are within each of us. My curiosity is piqued.

Filipe's home, an old adobe passed down from his grandmother, has plain brown walls with a few hanging retablos. Kerosene lanterns, handcrafted pots, special rocks, and mementos are on the window sills. Through the arched doorways, one can see long tables. Filipe, a potter, is soft-spoken, gentle, centered, earthy, his feet in soft-soled moccasins, his hair pulled back into a ponytail. He tells us that he is cooking beans and fried bread for us tonight. Usually he leads the sweat, but since a large workshop is coming the following day, Hildy, a tall, thin, blond woman with a German accent, will be the leader tonight. She explains in precise detail the working of the sweat, entering and exiting, using sage if you feel overwhelmed by heat, the stages of the ritual. I begin to relax.

We undress. Some of the women change into loose saris or wraparounds. Around the blazing fire, Hildy and her assistant Lisa brush negative energy off us one by one, with a feather dipped in smoke. Then she enters the low-built adobe lodge, and we follow. Kneeling to enter, I say, "To all my relations," and she hands me a sprig of sage. I choose a place about a fourth of the way around, close to the door but not next to it. Michael has chosen not to enter the sweat but to stay outside by the fire.

Heated rocks are brought in on a shovel to a deep pit in the earth. The door is shut. We are in total darkness but for a faint glow of the heated rock. Lisa leads us in a simple chant with a drum, blessing the Holy Father and Mother. Hildy prays to the Spirits of the East, the place of beginnings, which this round is dedicated to. I am already sweating profusely.

Seated between two young men, listening to the prayers and hiss of steam as water hits the rocks to bring the prayer into spirit form, I feel like an elder with tenderness and compassion for not just the two on either side of me but the entire circle. I don't feel too hot but enjoy the sweat dripping off me, all the impurities purging into

Mother Earth. If I lie back against the adobe wall, it feels cool. Hot in front, cool behind. The sensation is pleasant.

When the bowl comes to me, I think of many reasons to give thanks and ask for special blessings for my best friend and her daughter, who is fighting heroin addiction, and special blessings for my partner. The heartfelt sympathy in the circle is almost palpable as Hildy tosses water on the rocks to escort my blessing heavenwards or as steam to fall back upon us.

At the end of the first round, I step out, rinse myself with cold water, and join others around the fire. Buck and Filipe are firetenders. Others who decided not to do the sweat are holding the energy for us as we emerge. The night is beautiful. Sometimes gentle raindrops fall; sometimes the wind picks up. Behind a restless cloudy sky, the full moon is rising. Coyote moon. I squat by the fire, continuing my prayers in silence, feeling wild, organic, and free. After each round, more people crawl out of the sweat. The firelight glistens on their softened bodies. Their faces are filled with firelight and joy. I doze off and awaken to Filipe inviting people to come and eat. A feast awaits us of beans, fried bread, and chili, as well as chicken, green salad, coleslaw, watermelon, potato salad, and lemonade. I serve a peach cobbler I brought. Later I tackle the dishes, Filipe's grandmother's assortment, and immediately am joined by three women from our workshop. We work quickly and efficiently as a team, but it is two in the morning before we crawl into our sleeping bags.

The morning starts slowly. Under the blazing moon I haven't slept well and am grateful for the cup of coffee Michael brings. I dip a bit of leftover cake into it. We gather to share the impact of the previous night's sweat. Everyone looks relaxed, radiant, in a state of grace. Then Buck elaborates on the next part of our journey, the medicine wheel.

He and Hildy built it by intuition, resembling a labyrinth or the wheel of fortune tarot card. It is for us to experience individually as we wish. One quadrant represents Father and another Father's Ancestors, across is Mother and Her Ancestors. Beyond them, the Little Boy and Little Girl, and behind, the Warrior and Warrioress. He explains how all of these archetypes are in each of us. "Walk to where you feel pulled to go," he explains. "You may want to speak to an aspect of yourself. You can do all the wheel or only parts." We dress in ritual garments, T-shirts with saris or skirts. I have brought a purple T-shirt with coyotes on it and a special piece of silk from Thailand. Michael's hesitation about going down to the wheel and his exhaustion keep him from joining us. I move down to the wheel, picking up two small stones on the way.

Buck places a drop of oil on our third eye and says, "May your third eye be opened to experience the Wheel." Rowena baptizes our bowed heads with water. Once again we enter an altered state beyond definition, beyond time and space.

I am a little tired and disoriented as I approach the quadrant of Father and drop a heart-shaped stone. I have never felt close to my father's side of the family. But I choose to honor them, thanking them for their heritage of hard work, honesty, and humility. Then, thinking I will proceed to the Mother's side, the wheel leads me elsewhere. I notice the careful pilings of rocks, tiny yellow snapdragons, a design that seems organic and flowing and not like labyrinths I have walked before. I kneel in a circle that speaks to me from the Warrioress. Instantly an image comes to mind of a butterfly crawling out of its cocoon and straddling a leafy twig. I know if the butterfly doesn't dry its wings, it won't be able to fly and will die. I think of how strong I need to be to take care of myself, to protect the fragile delicacy of the emerging butterfly, and at the same time to take care of my partner. I begin to weep, softly at first, then from what feels like a deep well, grief, fear, and pain come pouring out. What feels like an endless rain of tears falls onto Mother Earth.

Eventually I leave the wheel to sit in the shade of a tall cottonwood tree. A dog that followed us from Felipe's home lies at my feet, as if to protect me. I touch her soft fur for comfort.

Buck leads us in a mediation of the wheel. He then invites us to act out some of our experiences of the wheel, speaking from the character we encountered. I find myself standing up and, in between sobs, speak my truth. It is the first time I have admitted my vulnerability to others. I always project the Warrioress image of strength, courage, and hopeful optimism. I say aloud, "I know my faith is unshakable. But I need to learn to receive as well as give." I describe the images that came to me and my process as unfolding "uncontrollably." I have an empathetic listening audience. Simply heard. Able to finish the words without interruption. What a gift. When I am through, Buck smudges me in a benediction with the smoking sage. When I sit down, Rowena tells me that a large monarch butterfly fluttered behind me as I spoke.

We finish our meditative storytelling with a prayer and a song, one that stays in my head for days, and then walk back to the house. We conclude our last circle by describing briefly our experience at the wheel. Then we take our candle and bless ourselves as we blow it out. Ours is already blown out again, and I relight it and explain how it keeps going out and getting relit. Michael blows it out, receiving the blessing.

We clean up the kitchen, pack, say farewell. I am feeling a little fuzzy at the edges and am in no hurry to get back to routine. Amazingly enough, it takes us four hours to get home, making stops and veering off on a scenic route to avoid a traffic pileup. A storm whips up, plunging us in a downpour that cleanses the car, the highway, the earth. I am cleansed and feel lightheaded for days.

And yet, I feel somehow incomplete, restless, uneasy. At my place of work, a hummingbird comes into the yard for the first time, reminding me of the hummingbirds that hovered at Buck's feeder. Then a week later, someone who was an important and special person in my life passes away, someone who represented the Trickster, the shadow side of a group we both belonged to. The lessons keep coming. I had been given signs of his death, signs I didn't understand. Only after the memorial's outpouring of stories through which forgiveness and healing take place do I feel that the work begun at the wheel has been completed. Only now, with my friend's ashes in a small urn in my hand, do I find peace.

I contemplate the messages of transformation and resurrection in the symbols that were around me during the Earthwalk weekend. I realize they were to help me understand not just the changes taking place in my own life, but also my heart's understanding of the ultimate mysteries. The prayer song comes back from the healing weekend: "Spirit of the wind, carry me home, carry me home to myself." And I feel that the way I walk on earth, my path in life, has altered, that I have returned to the center.

For ten years, WENDY L. BROWN lived communally, managing shelters for the homeless. A hospice volunteer, she studies alternative medicine and curanderismo. She has resided in Mexico, Spain, and Israel. Her writing group of five women has self-published *Dancing between Worlds*, a book of poetry, and performs in coffeehouses locally. Wendy's poetry has appeared in *Borderlands, Blue Collar Review, The Awakenings Review,* and *Moxie*. In the past year, she has become a widow and a grandmother and looks forward to publishing a novel about the ancient tribal worship of the Moon Goddess.

CAROL LEM

Shakuhachi and the Alhambra

*Music has power to ease tension
within the heart and to loosen
the grip of obscure emotions.*
—HEXAGRAM 16, YU

Maybe, it was the folds
of night and white noise,
the glowing Alhambra
on the next hill that made
the moment right.
I slipped my shakuhachi
from its warm case
and rubbed the dark bamboo.
While those, loosely
collected, talked and drank,
I propped myself on the ledge
of Mirador de San Nicolás,
crossed my legs, and blew
my first sound over the steep
cliff to the gardens of Spain.
As *Kyorei* floated in space
I was an *empty bell* drawing
a sudden hush around me.
Cameras flashed like stars,
but it was my instrument,
this Japanese flute against

a Moorish skyline that kept
me steady. And did I
imagine jasmine wafting
across the Eastern strains, or
was it as the *I Ching*
revealed in a dream, *invisible
sound* moves all hearts
and draws them together?
For when the last note faded
into the breeze, my companions
made a small circle, each
with a tale to empty, a *sound*
to add to all things unseen.

CAROL LEM teaches creative writing and literature at East Los Angeles College. Her poetry has appeared most recently in *Runes, Red Rock Review, Solo,* and *Rattle.* A poem and an essay on playing the shakuhachi (Japanese bamboo flute) as a meditation practice appears in *Wisdom of the East: Stories of Compassion, Inspiration, and Love.* Her books include *Don't Ask Why, The Hermit, The Hermit's Journey: Tarot Poems for Meditation,* and most recently *Shadow of the Plum.* Her work is also represented in *What Will Suffice: Contemporary American Poets on the Art of Poetry, The Geography of Home: California's Poetry of Place,* and *Grand Passion: Poets of Los Angeles and Beyond.* Her website is www.carollem.com.

PART IV

Community

The quality of our outer thinking
is determined by the depth and source
of our inner thought . . .
but quality from head to toe
depends on the quality of our life's love . . .
Heavenly love, with its desires for what is good and true
and the perceptions they prompt . . .
is like a tree's branches, leaves, and fruit.
The life's love is the tree; the branches and leaves
are the desires for what is good and true
and their perceptions;
and the fruit is the pleasures
of those desires and their thoughts.
—EMANUEL SWEDENBORG
   Divine Providence (paragraphs 106–107)

ART STEIN

Oranges

Morning at the Co-op   two women
embrace by the fresh produce   their
broad gestures and smiles signaling
the joy of an unexpected meeting
and they are beautiful

They move along the aisle sniffing
stem ends of melons and pineapples
their baskets turning slowly into
colorful still lifes   their alto/
soprano exchanges occasionally

interrupted with laughter as when
passing the daikon radishes   My
still life "Eggplants with three cans
of pomodori pelati" builds also   one
yellow pepper   two red onions

a garlic bulb   carrots   parsley and
oregano   Looking up from my list I find
myself staring at the fine cameo before
me   heads turning at the thudding
cascade of my Valencia oranges spilling

from their net bag   scattering across
the floor like pool balls at the break
Blushing   I accept their help corralling
the fruit   stop short of thanking them
for lighting my morning

ART STEIN, a semi-retired architect, lives in Northfield, Massachusetts, with his artist spouse, Margaret. His tanka were used as part page headings in the 2002 Chrysalis Reader, *Chances Are* . . . A selection of Art's tanka are to be included in an international tanka anthology, published by Red Moon Press later this year. His poems have appeared in *BOGG, Sahara, Fauquier,* and in publications specifically devoted to Japanese forms written in English—*American Tanka, Black Bough, Frogpond, Raw NervZ,* and *Modern Haiku.*

M. GARRETT BAUMAN

Quiet Ponds
for Bob Herzog

Charles Ephraim Burchfield. *The Quiet Pond.* Watercolor, 30×20 in., 1934. University of Arizona Museum of Art, Tucson. Gift of C. Leonard Pfeiffer.

IN THE FAINT PREDAWN LIGHT, I slip away from my sleeping wife, pull on old clothes, and leave the house. Fallen leaves swish and crunch underfoot as I hike the trail to the pond. The leaves soon will be sodden and black, but right now they are less like worn-out summer than some new magic. Nature's great disappearing and reappearing act. Our two-acre pond is disappearing too, having shrunk to one-third its normal size in this dry season, exposing a wide band of its bottom, now brick hard and webbed with fissures like an old man's sun-baked face. I'm here before sunrise to shake off the stories my students tell me, stories that make me thrash at five a.m.

I'm a college professor who lives on seventy-four acres of isolated woods and creeks in New York State, but I commute to Rochester, where my college has an inner-city satellite campus. I know how privileged I am to have escaped the ghetto where I grew up—literally across the street from infamous Eastside High School in

Paterson, New Jersey, portrayed in the film *Stand By Me*. Although I return to my country retreat each day, there is no escape for my students. Yesterday, a thirty-year-old student wept in my office, grieving the death of his brother—shot by a rival drug dealer. Although his three brothers deal and use heavy drugs, Jamal has been clean for a year. He wipes his eyes and breathes deeply, manfully, to control himself. "They're all going to be dead soon! This is my second brother killed." Jamal abandoned gang life to attend college. He planned to disappear and reappear, as a new person. He sold his expensive clothes, stereo, guns, and glittering ground-effects car to finance his education. Now he washes his clothes in the kitchen sink, eats at soup kitchens, and fears he will not have enough money to scrape through his final semester.

Another student who embeds herself in my thoughts is Pamela, with her two chronically ill children. Her daughter with sickle-cell anemia requires emergency trips to the hospital every few weeks. Her thirteen-year-old son has had a colostomy and must wear a bag to contain his uncontrollable waste functions. A schoolyard fall or a punch to the stomach could kill him. Yet she sends him out each day because she will not allow him to disappear into institutions. "My boy's going to live as much as anybody in this world!" she told me. "If he dies tomorrow, at least he's going to live first." Pamela is a superb student—hungry to learn and to improve everything she does—but her hands shake like leaves about to drop. Her flesh has shrunken in the struggle to obey her hard will. This week I advised her to ease off her volunteer counseling for rape victims. If she became seriously ill from her frenetic pace, how would her husband and children manage? "But it's important!" she protested. "These women have no one. They're suicidal."

"Are you?" I asked.

That made her grin. "I've got an ulcer. I put my worry there; that way I know where it is."

Violence is routine among my students. One class was talking about a shooting yesterday when I entered the room. A half-dozen of them were riding a city bus as gang gunfire erupted in the street, and the bus driver—like some old Gaby Hayes stagecoach hand—kicked the diesel horses into high speed and careened around a corner to escape. My students dove to the floor of the bus and used their book bags for shields. "My math textbook'll stop anything," one boy said. Some of them laughed nervously; others clenched their jaws and stared grimly ahead.

After class, as I sat in my office and watched the honking traffic and bustling pedestrians pass below, I thought, how can any of us achieve enlightenment in such a world? Am I to transmit eternal truth or even mundane truths to people shaking in terror or exhausted with worry? How can Jamal or Pamela flourish in such dry, abused soil? That thought jarred me awake at five a.m. Teaching is my vocation, but today is one of those mornings when I know I am no Buddha, no wise rabbi. I lack the inner peace my students so desperately need from me. My monkey mind chatters with scenarios of failure. Jamal will lapse into drugs or be shot; Pamela will drop out to tend her son who will die and devastate her. A college education is thin armor against such threats.

That is why I'm at the pond now. Teachers have often come to water to look into themselves and learn. *Budh,* the root word of the great teacher's title, means "to awaken" but also "to fathom a depth, penetrate to the bottom." I hope to learn from my water, disappear into it for a while and reappear. Like my shrunken pond that will fill in spring, like my students who dare to remake themselves, a teacher must be reborn each season.

It promises to be a great day to be reborn. Today, late October at dawn in upstate New York, it's sixty degrees. Sixty! I should bask in this rare gift from the weather, absorb it into my bones. As the sun rises, the shrunken pond reflects the trees' reds and golds and the ether blue sky. The still water captures even the flutters of leaves.

I envy the pond's calm and purity of reflection because my own mind is more like the pond in spring when the surface ripples and roils. Silvery bass leap into the air for insects and slap back down. Their rings spread to the farthest edges, then roll back to the center. And, of course, there are water snakes—fat, four-feet long, and nasty. They swim with heads high, watching me—unafraid, perhaps wishing their mouths were larger. I suppose every pond must have a snake or two, just as each heart must.

But there are other demons in my little paradise too. Just a few months ago as a mallard family paddled across the pond, six vees spreading behind the adults and fluffy chicks, the last chick in line popped under water and disappeared. No peep, no thrashing marred the surface. I glimpsed the yellow-streaked face beneath the water. Turtles drag chicks by the foot to the bottom to drown and eat them. The parent ducks did not even notice. They do not count chicks or name them. But I do count my students and sometimes know them too well. They are stalked daily, and even this early in the semester, some have begun to disappear. Latoya, James, Natalie, Ramon. Their ghostly faces rise in my dreams as if from under water.

Let the pond's stillness teach me something better I can bring to the city. Most people, I suspect, often wish for such a day's pure peace. If everything would just be still so we could concentrate! If we could just be what we might be without interference. Imagine what Jamal might accomplish in school if he did not have to deal with former addicts banging on his door to demand bags of cocaine, if he did not dread that he contracted HIV during his years of using needles. Imagine what Pamela might do if she were not distracted by platelet counts and emptying bags of fecal waste. Imagine if my students' burdens did not distract me, what I might teach them. Why must chaos scream in our ears?

Here is the question: Would our purest voice sing if the chatter around us and inside us ceased? Maybe. Or maybe it wouldn't make much difference. I confess I've had more than most humans' fair share of quiet—a dozen summers free from work's turtles to think about "higher" things. Magazine assignments have let me kayak on foggy lakes at dawn and stand alone in a Caribbean rain forest beside a waterfall with only Arawak ghosts for company and call it "work." Yet here I am, as unsettled as a harried case-worker or stockbroker. The truth may be that our most distracting noise is ourselves, and, if we skim off the noise, we may disappear with it.

Over the centuries, teachers and others have withdrawn to lonely deserts, mountains, and ponds to prepare themselves to reenter the world—seven days beside the water under Buddha's tree of life. Yet while Buddha meditated there, he was beset by a squalling demon that tried furiously to distract him from tranquility and understanding. This demon I take to be his own mind. He had to wrest peace from the noise inside himself. Only then did he become the great teacher. That is what I must learn.

I squat on the hardened mud shore to examine the water more closely. On the bottom, leaves have settled into brown ooze to be absorbed into next year's pond weeds. It is a model for transformation. I bend my face nearer the water to study the leaves below, furry with silt. There, an inch-long mayfly nymph rolls a dead leaf into a tube around itself for winter. In spring, it will emerge, rise to the surface, and fly. It seems like another lesson—teachers must be shape-shifters to help others transform themselves. We must change from the inside out if we are to leave the mud and enter the air. As I mull this over, I spot a dragonfly nymph hunting the mayflies under water. It too will grow wings under its chitin shell this winter and fly next spring. When it locates a mayfly, the dragonfly unrolls the leaf and seizes the nymph about the middle with powerful jaws. The mayfly twitches feebly as the dragonfly eats it. There is going to be more to this than I thought. Enlightenment doesn't come in safe doses.

In one of those magical optical revelations, my eyes adjust, and I realize I have been staring at the silty bottom right through the image of the moon floating like a lily pad on the water's surface. I glance over my shoulder to the moon in the sky—as faded and unreal as its watery image. Surely it must be even more serene and still than my little pond. No wind stirs the human footprints left in its dust decades ago. No pond dragons or snakes squirm there. No messy lives, no industry, no war shatters the lunar silence. But its quiet luminescence is deceptive, my niggling brain instantly reminds me, for its light is the reflection of thousands of hydrogen explosions on the sun. That is a neat trick—to transform utter holocaust into ethereal light.

But what if we look at the earth from space too? What of our turbulent, teeming masses and their teeth-clenching pain? Our blue-and-white globe floats in a quiet pond too—the Milky Way—whose millions of suns and planets, like a thin strand of algae, barely disturb the vast pools of space. From such a perspective, the sun's violent fits are mere twinkles on the water, and the earth's convulsions and my students' miseries no more than protoplasm streaming in a cell. Once in a while, a supernova ripples the weeds in a far corner. Otherwise, we scarcely notice the magnificent silence of light years around us, so deafened are we by our own petty noises.

If I could enlarge my mind, I might see the violence of my students' lives from such a perspective. The moon and sun, the leaves and pond, the flesh and blood, and the grief and rapture of humans rise and fall in seasons, in endless death and rebirth. Just like quiet and noise. If we have noise now, we will have quiet later. A quiet pond now, a raucous city later.

We who are living are each the single survivor of hundreds of eggs and millions of sperm. Each of us has won a lottery against incredible odds. Perhaps we ought simply to be thankful for the privilege of crossing the emptiness to hear and feel anything. I will remember this when Pamela phones me with a question from the hospital where she's writing her next paper while her moaning daughter endures an excruciating blood transfusion to treat her anemia. I will celebrate her energy and defiance of silence, not pity her. To feel anything is a gift. Jamal fears he has AIDS from years of drug abuse but cannot bring himself to be tested. Perhaps I should remind myself that he is lucky to have lived at all. That all the living die, and all the dead will be reborn. Should I tell him the great quiet will come, and there will be no more threats or lost brothers? I must give him something from this glorious dawn.

The sun pushes its glittering fingers through the tree branches and the moon is evaporating, almost gone. Gone? That thought snaps me to greater attention. No. It will still be there, although I will not see it when the sun beats the sky like a drum. The moon will simply be invisible, disappear. Even on the other side of the earth, the moon is still there. The cycle of day and night exists only in our limited human perception. The sun shines steadily every hour of every day; night exists only behind the earth's shadow. Just as we create darkness when we block the light. Perhaps when we imagine tranquility/disaster or life/death as polar opposites, we are mistaken in just such a way. The pond and the whole earth float in the sky, part of it, not apart from it. Just as my students are here with me, reflected in everything I see today. When I talk with them later, what I have seen here will light my words, even if I say nothing about this dawn excursion. This morning light will illuminate all the shadows I step into—or cast—today.

So here is a conclusion: There are no irrelevant noises, no distractions, and we have no pure self that can live separately from what surrounds us. My discomfort this dawn may simply be reluctance to allow my students' noise and pain into my quiet country life. I want to continue to think of myself as one who escaped the ghetto. But I mistake the cure for the sickness. To be separate is not to be safe but rather to be most in danger, most ripe for misery. This is not easy to say when one cherishes solitude as much as I do. But when I accept the noise of Jamal and Pamela's pain and my own, I believe I will hear the quiet.

Beside a half-dead maple tree—one side holed by woodpeckers, the other hung with yellow leaves tipped scarlet—I sit in the sunny grass. It will serve me as well as Buddha's Bodhi tree. The moon has melted into the sunlight. I lie back and breathe in the balmy breeze— the breath of summer in the mouth of winter. These same molecules have passed through the lungs of the great teachers. I inhale it so I can breathe it out later, in the city. I do not know yet what I will tell my students or how exactly I have changed, but we will learn together and then forget together, for knowledge disappears and reappears the way pond, moon, seasons, and humans do. Jamal and Pamela teach me to embrace risk and transformation, to treat education as the adventure it is, to grasp at this fleeting life with passion. For the moment at least, I know that even the pain is full of wonder and luck, and that each day offers a thousand joys we pass by as we seek our misery. Perhaps I can help my students to see and listen better for the joys. The whining buzz of cicadas, squirrels arguing over a hickory nut, the din of a class debating the needle-exchange program, and the furor of hospitals and gangs stir like fetuses within the womb of quiet. Yet underneath, new silences incubate. Noise is the shadow of stillness, and stillness the shadow of noise. It is dawn now and time to go. I return the invisible moon's smile and breathe slowly. Slowly. As slowly as a mayfly rises to the surface.

M. GARRETT BAUMAN was born in an inner city and now lives a mile from the nearest road. His essays appear frequently in The Chrysalis Reader as well as in *Sierra, Yankee, The New York Times, The Chronicle of Higher Education* and many literary reviews. His book on writing, *Ideas and Details,* is in its fifth edition.

NINA ROMANO

Bread

Before dawn Nico and I stood in line in the one general store
on the Island of Ist. Roll call of the longest list of Slavic

names I've ever heard was ticked off. When all had bread tucked
under arm, then we—sojourners—could buy if any remained.

One day when there was not a single scrap, not a loaf left,
an old man with two sold us one of his, patting Nico's cheek.

Weeks later arriving at Korkula, a fat lady stopped singing
in her window; puffed red cheeks mapped spidery, smiled at Nico.

I admired her basil plants on the sill behind wrought-iron
freshly painted, so she picked and handed me a bunch.

Sunday everything's closed on the island town of Marco Polo.
I spoke to her in Sign—not a simple task with my baby in tow,

so I pointed to his ribs, touched his mouth, rubbed his belly,
cupped my hands, drawing them apart quick-quick—

the international sign for bread. She sent me to a nearby bar
and there an angel dressed in sailor suit, spoke Italian

to me. The sailor's Slavic, almost good as my Sign,
convinced the owner to give me yesterday's

fragrant-wood-burning-stone-oven-baked bread.
Zero dollars, zip dinars, zap lire. "Regalo, per favore."

We shook hands. I thanked him for the gift. He tousled Nico's
hair; we waved, passing though the lintel of an ancient door.

NINA ROMANO earned an MFA in creative writing from Florida International University in 2001. Her fiction and poetry have appeared in *The Rome Daily American, Gulf Stream Magazine, Grain, Voices in Italian Americana, Vox,* and *Irrepressible Appetites.* In 1997, Romano won first place in FIU's Graduate Poetry Prize. In 2000, she received honorable mention for the Christopher F. Kelly Award for Poetry (Academy of American Poets) and will be included in a Russian-American anthology edited by Dr. Anya Krugovoy Silver.

THE RIGHT REVEREND FATHER
ARCHIMANDRITE RICHARD WEINKAUF

In the Blink of an Eye

God winks are such things as meeting certain people you hadn't seen in a long time, going in a direction different than what you had planned, finding yourself in a situation you never anticipated.
—SQUIRE RUSHNELL

LIVING AND MINISTERING AS AN ORTHODOX MONASTIC PRIEST, I can experience doubt and lack of self-worth. In such moments, I cry out, "God! Did you call me to priesthood? If so, why?" On September 11, 2001, 9:30 AM, however, God winked at me right over my television set, interrupting the weather report that I always watch. My immediate response was that of a fireman; I felt a surge of adrenaline and had a clear understanding of what I must do.

Already in my monastic garb, I grabbed my sacramental stole and oils and went the four blocks to Saint Vincent Hospital. This place would be my base of combat ministry, my entrée into the bowels of hell, the likes of which I had only read about. After all, this work was what I was trained to do in the military and what I now do as priest. This time, were I to die, it would be in service to God and those in His image and likeness.

I arrived in front of Saint Vincent's and saw that their emergency plan was in full operation, extending out into Seventh Avenue. There were only two traffic lanes left for arriving ambulances. All available doctors, nurses, and technicians were on the street waiting to receive the wounded. We kept waiting, but only a few ambulances arrived

with firemen and police, all suffering from heart or lung problems. In the early hours, we were unaware of the facts of the terrorist attack. Long tables of food, water, soda, and even cake had been set up for all who were in need. These items came from the hospital, next-door neighbors, and coffee shops.

I was feeling sorry for myself as I found no one to raise from the dead. Just then, I ran into both my old friend, Father Roger, and a new friend and co-worker, Father Damien, who was from some island, the name of which I don't recall. He was a bishop, complete with ring and staff, yet insisted on simply being called "Father." The three of us became attached at the hip. Father Roger told us we should go to the New School, just two blocks away, where relatives were being interviewed to find lost loved ones.

After some time, we went back to the front of the hospital but found the same scene of prayerful waiting. The horrific reality we could hear across a pocket radio had not yet been revealed or realized in this place.

As a priest, I have often said that I do not chase after an ambulance to save a person's soul. But God winked, and low and behold, a big white-and-yellow ambulance pulled up right in front of me with the backdoors wide open. No one was inside. I asked the driver, "Where is the patient?"

He said they had been delivered to the waiting doctors. He was to take back fresh supplies for a new triage site.

Father Damien looked at me and said, "Let's go where the souls need us."

I said, "Father, you are out of your head. I am seventy-one and a recovering heart-attack patient. You are using a cane." I had to think fast. Do I really believe what I preach? Do I want to walk the walk or just talk the talk? I looked at Father Damien. He was smiling, and then I smiled too, as little boys do. I said, "Let's do it."

In the tradition of those who go into battle, we blessed each other. Some young medical students pushed us into the ambulance, up over boxes of bottled water, masks, candy, apples, and bandages. I listened as the others in the ambulance told me how to put on a dust mask and about the danger in front of us. I asked, "Is this any way to treat an old priest?"

The ride down to what was to become known as "ground zero" was slow, rough, and jolting. The street was covered with debris, steel, and rock fragments. The air was quickly contaminated with pungent, unfamiliar, scatological odors of destruction. My remembrance of the killing fields in Korea, though, caused me to identify that universal smell—death.

Opposite:
Bernice Cross
Stone Angel.
Oil and sand on canvas,
24×14⅛ in., 1950.
The Phillips Collection,
Washington, D.C.
Acquired 1950.

GOD'S FIRST WINK FOR ME WAS MY BIRTH in 1930. I looked around and saw a light too bright for me: two parents, German and Polish, and a society in financial depression. I realized this human experience might be tough, but it just might work for me.

God's next wink happened when I entered the first grade at Saint Monica School. I was under the control of eight nuns for eight years. Each had two hands, but within the right hand was the growth of a twelve-inch, light-brown ruler. Each inch was named after an apostle of Jesus Christ. Now that scared me.

The next wink of God was when my very best friend in eighth grade told me I must go with him to the first seminary established in America by the French Holy Cross Father Isaac, a place then-connected with the University of Notre Dame at South Bend, Indiana. I was to be a priest. I thought this would be great for me, as Jesus was sweet, and his Holy Father would not be like my own heavy-handed father. So off we went to the "Angel Factory." It was not very different from my parental environment, which was stern, secretive, and a place where I remained under surveillance at all times. Father Holy Rector and the twelve priest teachers morphed, just like those sacred nuns of earlier days, into my German father. It would be impossible for me to ever give witness of them smiling, laughing, crying, or giving a nod of approval to me or to anything else outside of themselves. "O God, save me, from these holy and pure men."

You guessed it, God winked, and I audaciously climbed over the seminary wall. Within two weeks, my government informed me that the military exemption for the seminary had ended. I was expected to defend and protect my country from communist Korea. They placed me in the U.S. Air Force. They thought it made sense. I had been educated in an "Angel Factory"; therefore, I should fly.

My soul was in torment. How can I kill God's grandest creation? In a bomber, I will be an angel of death—not of life. This thought became a moral ethic that would stay with me all my life. I earned U.S. Air Force medals, but the big ribbon for good conduct was the one that made me laugh. With eight nuns, twelve priests, and my parents, what else but good could come from me?

After four years, I was released from active duty in the air force. That last night, as an airman, I had a restless sleep, full of dreams about liberation and personal freedom. No more killing. No "yes, sir" or "no, sir." No more taking orders. I would be in control of my life at last.

Looking back through the years, I now understand why I chose to be a biblical prodigal son. With government discharge money, good looks, strong health, and a need to make up for the past years, I took a train to New York: Broadway, show biz, wine, women, song, and dance. Yes, I became a song-and-dance man. "Look out world," I said, "I am in control."

As a government-paid student in the American Theaters Wing, it was exciting to perfect my natural talents. But with my background of the military, seminary, nuns, and my over-vigilant parents, I was too much a scrupulous prude. I never got a big part. I thought I was a failure. So I looked for a wink from God. But I guess a prodigal son does not experience a "god wink." It was degrading to be recognized as a failure. So, I just trolled the streets of life, taking jobs that did not need my skills or faith.

Quickly I became overqualified for every twelve-step program there was. After a few years, God winked again. It was a dark, cold, wintry night. I was in the only place I felt secure, accepted, and understood: my usual bar with my only true friend, Bob the bartender. During one of our often politically incorrect diatribes, Bob informed me that I knew nothing about the history of Constantinople or the Orthodox Christian Religion of Eastern Europe. Bob was correct. So the next night, along with a free beer, came two four-inch-thick books on the Byzantine Empire. This was the next wink of God.

I had held a secret throughout those years, unknown even to my few friends: I had taken extension courses in Christian Theology, Metaphysics, Comparative Religions, Psychology, and Spirit Healing. These studies were more than would be required of any priest, but I never planned to do anything professional with them.

God winked again. This time, an Orthodox bishop was talking to me and told me I must be called to the priesthood. My reply was "Not me, I'm a prodigal son."

The bishop replied sternly, "Good! They make the best priests."

About a year later, I found myself somewhere in Lower Manhattan walking the cold streets. It was noon. I had just left a friend's loft where fifty of us had drunk through the previous night. The only thing we had in common was drinking, and we shared no belief in anything but our own self-importance. I had been the last to leave. I had only one dollar in my pocket and a big need to find a toilet. I may have been drunk, but the real pain was inside my soul. I truly believed what I had studied, what I had starved and sacrificed to learn about during the hidden, secretive years of research into "real life." Who would believe me? How could I teach or use what I had learned? I came upon a small, narrow, four-story building centered in a block-long parking lot. It was painted pure white and had one wooden door with a small wooden cross on top. There was a small sign on the outside of the building with words written in a foreign language. But I recognized the words "church" and "Saint Nicholas." Just then, the door opened and out came a lady who smiled at me as she said, "hello," holding the door open for me to enter. I went inside, relieved myself, and rested in that warm building for some time. The service in progress was in Greek. It was so rich in color, smells, bells, and the bright icons of people of wholeness—the saints. Not one human spoke to me, but in English I clearly heard: "You are my priest forever." I cried and quickly left the church in disbelief. I must be nuts.

Another year later, I was ordained an Orthodox priest and monastic missionary to the "unchurched." I would go to these people wherever God called me. The poor, sick, and socially rejected call me "Father" and request the sacraments. I do my best with no financial support. My friends are too poor, but their greetings of "Thank you, Father" and "God Bless you, Father" are rewarding. I understand that the more affluent have their own priest, and that's good.

THE AMBULANCE STOPPED AT LAST, and the gates to hell opened wide. We climbed out and into a vortex of ghoulish gray dust, made up of a trillion computer papers, plastic lunch bags, and very personal effects. The dust was in and on all the trees, buildings, crushed fire and emergency trucks, and thousands of private cars. The firemen with their hooligan hooks looked like distorted, uniformed characters from Mars. In twenty-two minutes, I too was covered: my robes, my hair, and inside my mouth. I never knew there was a taste to terror: the dust of the world's largest outdoor crematory.

A medical student called us over to an open space under a ledge formed by the overhang of a damaged building. An abandoned hooligan hook was shoved into a very large crack to hang the precious bags of saline solution which were used to wash out the fine ground contaminants which blind the eyes. We received our first walking but sight-impaired firemen.

I went out into the area and pulled on one fireman's coat sleeve and ordered him to follow me to our triage. The firemen walked in small, supportive groups, so, if I got one, I got them all. I demanded they remove their dirty, dusty helmets and form a single line. I said, "Close your eyes," and I washed their dirt-caked faces. Then I said, "Open your eyes," and I washed their eyes out. I gave them a bottle of water, an apple, or a candy bar. It was their choice. During these close, intimate face-to-face relationships, as a mother to her baby, I saw their faces as the incarnate Christ. Their eyes, eyes of eternal life, reflected a litany of death, loss, hope, helpless courage, and a terror beyond feelings. Through all of these came the overpowering and eternal love of one for the other. Truly, in the giving is the receiving.

Some asked me for a blessing or even wanted to confess. In humbleness, I obliged. As the firemen walked back to their dangerous work with renewed vision and untangled souls, I received their benedictus, "God bless you, Father."

Then it happened, a message came from my God in the form of an angel. This good-looking man stood right in front of Father Damien and myself and said, without introduction, "Follow me but stay within my light. I'll take you to the morgue."

Father Damien looked to me and said, "How could he know what we really came down here to do?"

I was impressed with the the stranger's cleanliness, especially his shoes. No one there had clean shoes. The angel moved fast. His light illuminated our path in front of us yet also behind him. We stumbled along in his very large circular light for five blocks in that morbid atmosphere of manmade cosmic destruction.

Suddenly, both the angel and his light disappeared. We were in front of the large doors of a dark, damaged building. There was only a small generator supplying light on the inside of what seemed to be the elegant lobby of a café from another time.

As I stood there, I heard and saw a very old, black, dirty, long refrigerator truck: a temporary morgue. It's driver stood next to it. This electrical mausoleum was surrounded by firemen standing and sitting. They were tired, dejected, and overwhelmed by the magnitude of destruction and death, all of them focusing on the dirty truck. As Father Damien and I came closer, some of the firemen came to us, offering the salutation, "God bless you, Fathers." They escorted us to the small, rickety platform that raised us to the truck's flooring. Their flashlights helped us to see the red body bags. We loudly intoned the ancient prayer for the dead. They told us not to open the bags, making it sound as if the bags contained a secret. As we departed that scene of reverence and respect, I heard a chorus of a deep-toned, "God bless you, Father."

Just then the angel made another welcomed appearance and silently directed us to once again walk in his light. The angel's clean light led us into the dark, dusty café lobby. We slowly shuffled our way through debris, passing rescue workers and large tables of water, apples, and those big candy bars. Young men and women were serving it all with a smile. As we passed them, they smiled and said, "God Bless you, Father." We continued in our faithfulness to the angel's light.

Father Damien moved on ahead of me at some distance. I had to stop to think. Then I noticed to my right side a long table covered with a clean, white covering draped to the floor. Over each end of the table hung a light bulb. Next to the table, on the floor, there was a tall stack of red body bags with shining brass zippers. The area all around this table was swept clean suggesting this was a different kind of place. I saw two adult acolytes approaching in a short procession, their hands carrying the offering for a liturgy: a sacrifice to God. Sanity took over. I knew, and quickly had to accept, that coming into this place, soon to be consecrated with blood, were firemen. They respectfully placed a long basket in front of me on the table. It held what looked like parts of a large, broken child's doll. Then I heard one fireman in his tearful voice, sounding like a deacon to me, say, "Bless! Father." He walked back for more. In this most unusual and exceptional moment of earth's history, I found myself standing alone doing what I thought some human would do for me, treat the remains of my body as the container of my soul. I blessed the body parts and placed them into the bags. Here I was in a catacomb of a destroyed civilization, at an altar-table of the sacrificed.

After a long time, there were no more baskets of body offerings, just the incense of decay. A very intrusive, loud, and demanding voice jolted me back into the world of human authority and fear. It was Father Damien walking toward me with a tall policeman in pursuit, telling him he could not be in here for this was a crime scene. Father Damian stopped and turned, placing his old gold-ended cane in the officer's chest, and said as only a saintly priest could say, "Crime scene? This is God's scene." The officer left us alone. The angel made an unexpected reappearance and told us it was time to return to our triage center. It seemed to be daybreak with more rescue workers and clergy arriving.

Back at the triage, a fireman whom I had prayed with the night before came to me with his helmet in his hand and said, "Father, last night you wanted to know if St. Nick's Church was okay. I have to tell you that it is destroyed, down to the ground." He saw me cry and held me in his strong, supportive arms. The ambulance from St. Vincent's came by, and the driver offered to take us back to the hospital.

After a hot shower and a light meal, we ran into Father Roger again. We told him what we had experienced. He wanted to go back down again. So we did, this time in a FEMA bus. We arrived at the same triage site and started all over again. We even went back to that mausoleum. It was the same scene but with even more firemen, and all three of us stood at the truck which was now full, and we blessed the bodies.

As we started back to the triage, the most loud alarm sounded with all the firemen, police, and rescue workers running away toward uptown. All passed me by. Someone said that the number five building was about to tumble over on us now! I walked as fast as I could. I was so afraid. Not to die but to be seen as an old man. The building didn't fall, and all the workers went back into the pit of wind, fire, and the sting of death. Since we three old, dirty, tired priests had already run or walked four blocks out of harm's way, we decided to keep walking uptown toward the fresh, clean air and sunlight.

We each walked in silence. On that long walk back to civilization, I made a sacred vow to God, the blessed Trinity, and to St. Nicholas: I would return to Ground Zero on the very spot where the Church of St. Nicholas stood and give public praise with prayer, smells, bells, candles, and thanksgiving to St. Nicholas. This church was the same spot where, twenty some years ago, God called me to the priesthood. I vowed to proclaim God's grace on all my "firemen of God" and my angel, wherever he may be. Praise God, I did it. Four months later, on the eve of St. Nicholas' saint's day, with the help of New York City Police Officer Lee of the 1st Precinct, I was able to keep my vow.

I gave this report to my bishop, just last week. My bishop said, "Now! Do you trust God? Hundreds of firemen spoke to you for God and said 'God bless you, Father.' How can you even doubt your priesthood or the need for you as His priest?" Right then in my ear, God winked. I understood at last. I am a priest forever. Thank you, God, and bless your messengers, the police and firemen, at that place that Father Damian named "God's scene." True! It was all in a wink of God's Eye.

THE RIGHT REVEREND FATHER ARCHIMANDRITE RICHARD WEINKAUF still resides in that inner desert of chaotic Manhattan. In his monastic quarters of the anchorite lifestyle, he continues to seek knowledge of the existence of and need for a God, let alone a relationship. Father Richard's eclectic philosophical interests include the teachings of Jesus, Talmud, Upanishad, Swedenborg, and Madame Blavatsky.

TIM KAHL

The Exit Tamer
for Frank Dillon

He's the guy who taught me how to
drive in high school, made me do it right.
He taught me about speed,
eighty-five on the back roads to
Canal Fulton. The bumps made us fly.
I'd take the Pontiac out and practice speeding
until I told myself that I believed in it.
But my appetite was short-lived,
and now car sickness is always
looming, a vague threat
like sudden imprisonment for
past wrongs I've done to friends.

He drove me to high school every day,
showed up in a dozen different cars before
we reached graduation. He was always dealing.
There were trips to used car lots
and police auctions with him,
trips to parts stores in Massillon, trips to
softball practice and the fish fry afterwards,
trips to miniature golf where everyone
cheated on their score. There was no way of
knowing who might face punishment
for such meaningless deception.
There was no way of knowing that
by the time I had my degree, he'd be
matriculated into the void's dark institute.

I saw him last at his parents' house.
He was in the final months of regressive Hodgkins.
He joked that he was eating enough rice cakes and
yogurt for him to live to be a hundred,
yet we both knew that was unlikely to happen.
When I left, I told him to take care of his collie.

It was an awkward departure. He wanted me
to look him in the eyes and put my trust in him
again. He needed me to believe what
he had learned about resignation.
He knew that exiting was a lot like taming lions
—one forces a ridiculous invincibility.

So many of the people I've known
have quietly resigned themselves to something.
They knuckled under to consequences
and held on. It is a survival strategy.
Otherwise there is crippling disappointment.
This is what separates the young from the old.
The old resign themselves to comfortable postures.
The young drive all night to reach Cleveland;
there they head south to arrive by morning
in Canton, where a collie stands in the yard alone
barking at the kids in the neighborhood
loading themselves onto the bus.

At the funeral I said my goodbyes to friends,
and that was the last time I left Ohio. I'm not that good
at leaving. There is always one more clever
remark to add. And when my last bit of errant wit
fell into useless silence, I had the whole trip
back to Michigan to reprimand myself,
to revisit the days of all of us playing euchre in
the kitchen, to retrace the paths some lives take.
I steered for Toledo. The hum of the tires on the turnpike
could have been his voice. His voice was a car horn
passing in the fast lane, confirming that it was
right there. I'm sure it was him. He was the guy
who always told me *we have to get off this exit here.*

TIM KAHL teaches at Sacramento City College. His work has appeared or is forthcoming in *Apalachee Quarterly, Gulf Stream, The George Washington Review, OnTheBus, Prairie Schooner, Fourteen Hills, Illuminations, SunDog: The Southeast Review, Madison Review, Berkeley Poetry Review, American Letters & Commentary, Midnight Mind, Spoon River Poetry Review, Nimrod,* and *Caliban.* Tim adds, "I am also currently working on translations of German poets Rolf Haufs and Christoph Meckel, and Austrian avant-gardist, Friederike Mayröcker's book of poems/novel, *Das besessene Alter [The Possessed Senior Citizen]* as well as a collection of contemporary Brazilian poetry and the poetry of José Saramago."

DAVID ZANE

The Holy Virgin of Chernobyl

IT WAS ALEKSANDR VOYNOVITCH who first saw the Holy Virgin of Chernobyl coming up through the smoke of Reactors 1, 2, and 3, and then settling herself on the silent chimney of Reactor 4, which had not been in service for many years. This sighting occurred while he was delivering milk to the People's physicists living in Quonset huts on the site. Although obliged by regulations never to reveal anything seen within a thirty-kilometer radius of the installation, it was no more than a day's ride through the Dead Zone before the whispering began.

Manya Glaznovna wanted to know if the Holy Virgin had spoken to him, and Aleksandr Voynovitch replied without hesitating that she had invited him to tea, having gathered some sprigs of fresh mint growing wild in the outlands, but that she hadn't had time to prepare a currant cake. In any case, the samovar was ready.

Verification would not be simple since Manya Glaznovna had no authorized pass to enter the zone, and Aleksandr Voynovitch knew well what he was risking in hiding her amongst his milk jugs under the canvas covering of his truck. He had cut a lateral slit so that she could look out without having to raise the tarpaulin. He would park his vehicle facing the tower, but in no instance was she to cry out in ecstasy or even make the sign of the cross from flat on her back, for the risk of fluttering the canvas or overturning a milk jug.

When Manya Glaznovna finally saw the Holy Virgin of Chernobyl, she had no desire to move at all. She lay in a kind of pleasant paralysis, fixing her through the torn canvas as she sat knitting a sweater on top of the reactor chimney. Manya Glaznovna would remember only the terrible thirst this induced in her, envying

Opposite:
Yves Tanguy.
From Pale Hands to Weary Skies [De Mains Pales aux Cieus Lasses].
Oil on canvas, 35⅝×28⅛ in., 1950. Yale University Art Gallery. Bequest of Kay Sage Tanguy.

Aleksandr Voynovitch who had been invited up for sunflower seeds and vodka.

Sworn to secrecy by Aleksandr Voynovitch, in fear of losing his milk route, Manya Glaznovna lay awake nights thinking about the Holy Virgin. Without needing to reveal what she had witnessed, it was soon enough seen on her being as she made her midwife's rounds in the makeshift rehousing centers. Touching an exposed belly with her hand while listening through her earpiece for the fetal heartbeat, she created an inadvertent electric shock. In one case, she actually induced labor. Every newborn she scooped into the world radiated an afterglow, and many opened their eyes before term at her fingers' beckoning.

ON THE DAY PEOPLE'S PHYSICIST LOPAKHIN saw three children at the site looking up at the huge chimney tower of defunct Reactor No.4, called the "sarcophagus" by those who knew its contents, he could not fathom how such a breach of security had been achieved. Dozens of kilometers around the site were frontiered by high, electrified barbed wire, and the only two points of entry were heavily guarded by army units. Also, it was a distance of over thirty kilometers to the nearest enclave, and it was inconceivable that they had trekked so far without being seen. Lopakhin was merely a finger's glide from the alarm button when he imagined the prescribed fate of these urchins: brutally scalding showers, shaven heads, and the loss of displacement benefits for their families who had been warned against letting their children play near the installation.

Yet his hesitation had another motive. He could tell—even from behind his triple-reinforced window—that the children had not moved since he first noticed them, merely staring up at some unidentified spot on the deactivated tower. And now, at ground level, Lopakhin could see more clearly that which had set his pulse racing from the laboratory window. The children had not budged and, even at his approach, made no effort to escape. He tried to press a coin into each small hand, but his thrusts were met by an uncanny heat, which set burning the metal he proffered. Passing his hand before their eyes, he got no reaction from the three sets of eyelids. And, at last, pricking their forearms with a pin, none of them registered the merest pain. Only when he tried to lead them to shelter did he meet any resistance. Despite his superior adult's strength, he could not deliver them from their chosen spot. Picking one of them up in his arms, he felt he was carrying an enormous weight, which caused him to clutch his lower spine and put the child down.

There was nothing else now for Lopakhin to do but enlist the aid of the installation's own doctor, specially trained in the effects of radiation phenomena. Together they examined the vegetative nervous system of each child still standing in place, measuring the cardiac rhythm, the capillary flux of the fingers, the electric resistance of the skin, as well as the respiratory rate. Attaching electrodes to their skulls, they took improvised electroencephalograms. With all of this data now passed through the central computer, the following diagnosis was reached: the patients were suffering from sympathetic hypertonia, a state of mental and physical alertness of extreme and dangerous intensity. Their cardiac rhythm attained a rate of 150–180 pulsations per minute as opposed to 67–75 in a normal, healthy individual. Tests made to the children's skin showed a complete absence of cutaneous resistance to stimuli, proving them to be completely insensitive to their surroundings, in sum, a phenomenon known to the People's scientists as the alpha state.

Kneeling down at the children's level, trying to incline his head at the same angle, Lopakhin found himself staring at the rim of the "sarcophagus." He wanted to be able to read their thoughts, to see with their eyes, yet nothing was visible to him but an empty sky. Besides, supposing there were something up there, the defunct tower being some forty meters high, it would have been impossible for the children to see it from the ground. Yet Lopakhin was determined to watch as long as they were watching. It was several hours before he saw it.

Lopakhin first thought what he saw was an optical illusion, but then it was very distinct in the lenses of his high-powered binoculars: a small bird, nothing more than a finch, flying round and round the rim of the tower, swooping and buckling, finally fluttering and plunging into the dead heart of the immense chimney.

While packing the children into the ambulance to transport them to the military hospital, Lopakhin saw hundreds of dusty pilgrims coming in the opposite direction. Why had the guards not turned them back at the checkpoint? A jeep full of soldiers followed, shouting warnings through a megaphone, but they moved at so swift a pace that no force could stop them. Only when they passed the area where most of them used to live did they turn their eyes away from the forward path. Several of the women began to wail and rush at the electrified fence but were stopped by others and dragged along in the direction of the towers.

Lopakhin stood down from the ambulance and pleaded with them not to go any further, but they simply jostled him aside. He suggested to the powerless soldiers following them that they send for mobilized reinforcements before the mob could reach the laboratories. When he turned around, he found that the children had fled the ambulance.

BY THE TIME THE COMMISSAR OF THE LOCAL KOLKHOZ, Viktor Kalinin, had arrived at the site in his limousine, the pilgrims had reached Reactor 4, but made no attempt to enter the now security-locked buildings. They sat in silent observation of the "sarcophagus," waiting for a sign from the Holy Virgin of Chernobyl, who was silent and unmoving, except for running a comb through her ankle-length hair from time to time, sending sparks into the air.

Viktor Kalinin knew each of these people by name and counted most of them amongst the inhabitants of the collective farm he administered. He himself had overseen the emergency re-housing and made sure that the new crop of orphans was fed by each family in rotation. Among them he noticed now several of the local "idiots," possessed by invisible demons, with long beards and eyes spinning like little birds in their shaven heads. Once forbidden to read from scriptural texts, these men now recited verses from a language no People's anthropologist could decipher, making Kalinin's task of integrating them into the workforce a herculean one.

But it was only when he saw the solitary onion hanging around the necks of numerous pilgrims that he began to understand. The Russian sinner knows that he must keep an onion about him at all times by which the Holy Virgin can pull him up into heaven at the moment of his death.

Viktor Kalinin, however, was more alarmed by the loss of a day's work than by the Holy Virgin of Chernobyl. For years, production quotas had been steadily decreasing, ever since the peasants were forced to farm land that had not been theirs since birth. No coercion could make them work faster; they were listless and unmotivated. Thus, it was Kalinin who alerted the Central Committee in Kiev, which phoned the Politburo in Moscow, which in turn ordered the army to get the situation in hand.

PEOPLE'S PHYSICIST LOPAKHIN, however, was not so versed in peasant tradition and had been trained in Party cells to combat superstition wherever it was met. All that afternoon, he had been taking readings of the "sarcophagus," and discovered a rate of radioactivity twenty times that of normal functioning. But how could this be? Reactor 4 had not been functioning for years. It could never be employed again after the sad meltdown had resulted in its being cooled, its interior then covered with concrete and sealed for at least two centuries of half-lifing. The funneled mouth of the dead tower was checked daily for leaks, but these had always been minimal. What's more, readings taken from the three towers of the functioning reactors were suddenly inferior to those taken at No. 4.

So, with dozens of armed squadrons ringing the kneeling pilgrims, eagerly awaiting the command to disperse them, Lopakhin asked for five minutes to address the crowd. He spoke to them through a microphone in one of the army vehicles, explaining that while science was powerless to determine the exact shape of what they claimed to be seeing, it could nonetheless prove that high levels of Cesium 137 in strong concentrations, although invisible and colorless, might just, given an unusual angle of solar rays, produce a kind of dance of particles filtered through ordinary dust carried on the air. Given certain atmospheric irregularities, it was not outside the providence of scientific law that certain visible, though incoherent, phenomena could result. Ergo: the Holy Virgin of Chernobyl was nothing more than a smattering of errant atomic particles and, as such, could perform no miracles.

When this wisdom failed to move them, the command was given for the military to sweep the pilgrims from the site. Saddened by the inexplicable failure of pure reason, Lopakhin went back to his laboratory, as the jeeps started up their engines. From his window, he was just in time to see the three children, not exactly climbing, but being borne up the concrete side of the giant reactor tower as if on invisible ropes, higher and higher until reaching the rim, then sucked suddenly, as if by aspiration, one hundred feet down into the dead heart of the "sarcophagus," causing dozens of birds to shoot out of it into the air, as out of an erupting volcano, spinning into formation and winging out over the Dead Zone.

ARMY MACHINE-GUNNERS COULD ONLY NEUTRALIZE so many of the pilgrims before being overrun. Viktor Kalinin, trying vainly to hold them back, watched as the remainder headed east-southeast, following the path of the finches. Some tried to scale the barbed wire fence, only to be electrocuted in the attempt. But one or two "idiots," like Aleksandr Voynovitch the milkman, took the current full force. With bare hands numbed by the Holy Virgin, they tore gaps in the deadly barrier to let others through.

With his binoculars Lopakhin could spot the finches from as faraway as the laboratory, saw them describing circles over contaminated land where once a human settlement had been. The houses there had to be razed to the ground, the soil turned under, the vegetation pulverized and covered over with durable plastic sheeting. This Dead Zone would be off limits for hundreds of years, would never grow a single weed again, and was mortal to anyone coming in contact with it. This is why army riot-quelling planes now swooped down on the arriving pilgrims and managed to spray them back out of the area with water cannons.

As the birds circled silently above her head, Aleksandr Voynovitch was the first to reach the Holy Virgin of Chernobyl, who was dressed now in lead overalls and hard plastic boots, breaking the soil with an army spade and urging the "idiots" to join her. Aleksandr was sure he recognized the very spot on which she was standing, even though the familiar trees were no longer there. He had played there as a boy and could tell now from the angle of the sun just where the finches had led them.

Below the feet of the Holy Virgin, buried under tons of sand and debris, lay the communal stone wash-house which formed the fulcrum of the little Ukraine town where he was born. Suddenly, Aleksandr Voynovitch understood why she had come all this way, and why she had sought him out in the first place.

Digging now with her, although unable to match her depth of shoveling, which could upturn ten feet of earth at a thrust, and despite the jets of the water cannon which continued to force him back to the fence, he pressed his spade into service wherever he could. This act of faith was to uncover the old town's primeval well where he used to drink fresh rainwater as a boy and where the Holy Virgin of Chernobyl had come from the other side of the world just to wash her soiled linen.

DAVID ZANE won the Pushcart Prize for "Hector's Letter," in *Missouri Review*, 1988–1989. His short fiction has been published in *Penguin Modern Stories, Partisan Review, New Directions, Tri-Quarterly, The Quarterly, Massachusetts Review, Chicago Review, Fiction, Missouri Review, Confrontation, PN Review, Chariton Review, Michigan Quarterly Review, Literal Latte,* and BBC radio fiction programs. A volume of stories, *In the Slipstream,* was published by Chicago Review Press. His other published books include *The Radical Soap Opera, Wilhelm Reich for Beginners, Introducing Kafka* (with Robert Crumb), *Introducing Camus, BAMN*. His articles have been published in *Harper's, Vogue, Village Voice,* and *Sunday Times* (London). His plays for theater and radio are regularly produced throughout Europe. He lives in Avignon in the south of France.

GARY SANDMAN

Quaker Peace Vigil

David L. Paffhausen. *The Urban Chronicle.* A suite of prints in collaboration with Jack Carlton. Etched in copper, 15×21 in., 1985.

ROCKING FROM FOOT TO FOOT, I stare down Fifth Avenue. I pass my hand over my balding head. Twenty people stand beside me. We're lined up in front of Washington Square Arch as witnesses for peace on a chilly April Sunday afternoon, black clouds overhead threatening rain.

I became a Quaker during the Vietnam War. Raised working-class Irish Catholic, appalled at the senseless carnage, I had applied for a conscientious objection to military service. I read *The Quaker Contribution* while researching the basis for my claim.

Intrigued, I attended a Quaker meeting and was soon drawn strongly to their practices of silent worship and applying their strong convictions in practical ways. A quiet, unobtrusive presence, Quakers have lived in New York City since the 1650s. Early English converts were beaten and jailed. When John Bowne, one of their leaders, was fined and imprisoned, he appealed to the Dutch West Indies Company. Its directors ordered that colonists be allowed to worship as they pleased. This was the first statement of religious freedom in America.

Over the centuries, Quakers here have been active in abolitionism, education, feminism, and prison work. Currently they operate Brooklyn Friends School; Friends Seminary, also a school; the Friends Cemetery in Prospect Park; the Fifteenth Street Meeting homeless shelter; and Friends House in Rosehill, a residence for AIDS victims. Perhaps five hundred members belong to the nine meetings or Worship Groups (fledgling meetings) within the city's boundaries; probably twice that many attend without formal membership.

Quakers from Fifteenth Street Meeting, the group in the East Village, have organized the vigil. I glance down our line. I know many of the people here. Most are Friends; some are not. A few appeared to have simply wandered up and joined us. Standing beside me, Christiana, tall and elegant beneath a wide-brim hat, clutches a big sign, and Lisa, a friend of Friends, pretty and blonde, sips juice from a bottle. Arthur, an older man, craggy, in an old seersucker suit, walks over and stands with us, leaning heavily on his cane.

Quaker nonviolence has been sparked by its practice of silent worship. Friends believe that God inspires them to speak and act in these quiet times. They call it the Inner Light or that of God within. A typical meeting for worship involves anywhere from a few to several hundred people gathered for an hour. Every so often someone offers a short message.

Over the years, I have felt led to become involved in the world from the Inner Light, this something stirring inside me during Quaker worship. It prompts me to take part in the vigil, this Worship in Action. Nowadays I attend the peace vigil occasionally, I serve on the pastoral care committee—the group in my meeting that provides practical support to Friends about such things as membership, marriage, and conflict resolution—and I spend a lot of time working with the Green Party on electoral races and community organizing projects. These are my ways of seeking a better world.

Margery, a handsome woman with wispy, gray hair, a Quaker for forty years and a civil-rights veteran, explains to a passerby why we're at the vigil. "Friends are concerned about violence, national and domestic, so we've struggled with this concern in many ways. We founded the Alternatives to Violence Program that teaches conflict resolution in schools and prisons, for example. And we've been holding a silent vigil at the Arch on and off since the Vietnam War."

My attention wanders. I inspect a pair of buildings looming over us to the left and right: light-gray One Fifth Avenue and dark-brown Two Fifth Avenue. The sky darkens; pigeons flutter onto the cornices of the townhouses opposite them. I zip up my light, black jacket to ward off the chill and lean back against the chain-link fence surrounding the weather-beaten Arch.

As people stroll by, they glance at our signs, respectful, curious. Occasionally one stops to speak to Margery, who has been delegated to answer questions, or takes a flyer from her. Some drivers honk or wave.

At a past vigil, a young man pranced up and down in front of the line, chanting, "I know you want to speak! I know you want to speak! I know you want to speak!" During another one, Yoko Ono and her friend Sam Havadtoy walked south on Fifth Avenue toward us. Ono stared suspiciously, studied a sign, then smiled and blew us a kiss.

A few raindrops spatter my old tennis shoes. A tourist snaps our picture, then moves on. Four teenage girls cross into the park, laughing.

New York City Quakers no longer dress like the Quaker Oats man or speak the plain language ("thou," "thee," and so on) like Gary Cooper and Dorothy McGuire in the movie *Friendly Persuasion*. Most dress simply, though, and some use the plain language with one another. They're used to people thinking that their religious society is extinct or that they're Amish.

What makes New York City Friends especially unique is their attempt to live as an oasis of calm in a frenetic city. They treasure their stillness. Even when Quakers are in conflict, their tradition urges a return to a cool, meditative center. It's a quietude born not of apathy or creed but of rock-hard conviction: to be continually aware of the presence of God.

With my many everyday commitments, it's a hard struggle to stay within that stillness. What helps me, though, is the Quaker testimony of simplicity. (Testimonies are beliefs Friends have discovered over the centuries and to which they try to live up.) Simplicity encourages me, among other things, not to take on too much. I'm wary of taking on extra projects, and, rather than be overwhelmed by them, I try to whittle them down as much as I can. Another help to that stillness is Quaker worship. That blessed hour of silence just lets me be present. And many years ago, from practice of the worship, I was able to take it with me out of the meetinghouse and into the world.

Finally, we gather in a circle with linked hands, still in silence. Then we break, chatting quietly. I say to people, "See you all next month." They nod, smiling. Rain begins to fall, umbrellas appear, and we scatter.

GARY SANDMAN, a member of the West Queens Greens as well as the Fifteenth Street Friends Meeting, is a writer and painter living in New York City. He has published articles in *Friends Journal* as well as the art history *Quaker Artists*. Currently, he is at work on two novels—*Resistance* and *Ceremonies*. He works as assistant manager at a group home for the developmentally disabled.

THOMAS R. SMITH

Trust

It's like so many other things in life
to which you must say no or yes.
So you take your car to the new mechanic.
Sometimes the best thing to do is trust.

The package left with the disreputable-looking
clerk, the check gulped by the night deposit,
the envelope passed by dozens of strangers
all show up at their intended destinations.

The theft that could have happened doesn't.
Wind finally gets where it was going
through the snowy trees, and the river, even
when frozen, arrives at the right place.

And sometimes you sense how faithfully your life
is delivered, even though you can't read the address.

THOMAS R. SMITH is a poet and essayist living in River Falls, Wisconsin. He has authored three books of poetry, most recently *The Dark Indigo Current* (Holy Cow! Press, 2000), with a fourth in the works. He teaches poetry classes at the Loft Literary Center in Minneapolis and writes criticism for the *Ruminator Review*. He believes that the quality of trust is essential to spiritual well-being, not to mention the making of poems.